Laughing in the light

JIMMY SANTIAGO BACA

Museum of New Mexico Press

Santa Fe

Director: Anna Gallegos
Editorial director: Lisa Pacheco
Art director and book designer: David Skolkin
Composition: Set in Minion and Helvetica Neue
Manufactured in United States of America
10 9 8 7 6 5 4 3 2 1

Library of Congress Control Number: 2019957223

ISBN 978-0-89013-645-4 hardcover
ISBN 978-0-89013-646-1 ebook

Museum of New Mexico Press
PO Box 2087
Santa Fe, New Mexico 87504
mnmpress.org

SUSTAINABLE FORESTRY INITIATIVE

Certified Chain of Custody
Promoting Sustainable Forestry
www.sfiprogram.org
SFI-01268

SFI label applies to the text stock

To the lovers of life, in all its myriad and contradictory delights.

Contents

Acknowledgments

I AM A HOST OF CONTRADICTIONS IN CONTINUAL FLUX, a moving target that changes shape from one moment to the next. The second you take your eyes off me and look again, I have changed, and while this continues to be true, the opportunities I've been given, used and wasted, ignored and plunged into headfirst, haven't changed. That's why there are so many of you reading this whom I wish to thank: first and foremost, always, my children—incredible spirits who gifted me with their laughter and love every single moment of my life. I don't exist without you.

I thank bookstore owners and book lovers, readers and poets, professors and healers, editors and publishers. My gratitude is unending, and not a day passes that at some moment in the day I don't incline my head and utter under my breath a thank-you prayer for your trust and belief in me.

If I have offended anyone or hurt your feelings, which I'm sure I have, I am sorry. I'm sometimes a boastful sonofabitch and at other times a most self-effacing and demure person, and those contradictions plague me, bounding me from loudmouth to shy listener, mouse who flees from a shadow to an outlaw warrior, incontinent and ascetic, incongruent and seamless, repentant to accuser, sacred to profane, courageous to coward: an assemblage of lightning strikes and candle flames, a desire to test and tempt death at every turn in the journey and a trembling, fragile, insecure man, retreating to his room to pray and beseech God to watch over me.

Being this person makes those who have loved me all the more amazing—how my children continue to love me, how they endured a poet as a father, an ex-con, a know-nothing but sincere husband, a half-wit farmer, a pathetic example of a hero, and still, in my inglorious faults and shortcomings, not a morning came when they didn't hug me and kiss my cheek and say, I love you Papi. (It's the strength of our *raza*, how strong we believe in la familia y nuestra cultura.)

There are many more who made me better for knowing them: Ben D., David M., Jeff D., Ron S., Grove, ND, the Museum of New Mexico Press, and those who first published me: Arturo S. in *Seer's Catalogue,* and when I was in prison Timberline Press, Rock Bottom, Curbstone, Will I. from Illuminations, Moser, J. Harrison, D. Johnson, all those convicts I wrote poems for in exchange for cigarettes and coffee (your critical eye gave no mercy but taught me much!), my readers all over the world, Daniel and Lucia, students at hundreds of universities, and teachers, thank you for your patience and trust and emails, your kindness has often kept me going when I sometimes felt I couldn't; my adorable and beautiful wife Stacy, a virtuous poet in her own right whom I leaned on so many times when I couldn't find the strength to stand on my own. I owe so much to so many, I have to lump you all together like a night sky filled with stars and admit that without you my dreams would never have come true and they have because of your generosity. If not for you, I wouldn't be here. You've given me life, hope, allowed my aspirations to come true. Under those terms, your value to me cannot be measured except by not disappointing you, to continue writing and living in a healthy manner as I have for a long time. And with a determined vow to keep raising myself up to face another day, to confront injustice and challenge racism and go out and teach illiterate kids and adults how to read and write, to keep true to myself and honor your trust in me, I will.

Unlike many professions, as a poet there's no going home after work— your life is your work and nothing about society suits you as a poet, your clothes and shoes faded and worn and uncomfortable, yet this poet's passionate love for language and poetry persists with every breath and step and moment of sleep and wakefulness and is dedicated to the life of poetry in some way. Convoluted, down, up, sideways and around in a circle, poems command me, make up my world, and there is no time when you're off; poems block out the sun at dawn, face the sun at night, they take you down and bury you, dig you up and allow you to walk among the living, always conscious that you don't belong, that you shouldn't be here; you often alienate the people you meet with your weird antics; you find yourself constantly afloat on this huge ocean of stimulation and sights and sounds and ideas and feelings and your job is to bring order enough to create a foundation for others to stand and observe life from, listening to Mozart or Bach, Hendrix or David Gray—there's no career, or résumé or networking, no, sadly, there's only getting lost and trying to find your way back, every day, trying to find yourself again, trying to find a balance so that you won't feel this incessant suffering of insecurity, this chaos that pierces your brain and heart like a bullet dipped in acid; it's not painful as much as it is a desire that consumes you, a desire to embrace all of it all at once and enjoy the ultimate epiphany of being with God again and again.

I know I can be an unbearable nuisance, I know that, that I am reclusive and a maddeningly wild romantic driven by an obsessive lust and hunger to devour the human and the divine. I know. The arousal to be one with a woman's heart and one with the tree and grass blade hardly subsides, and I find myself permanently mangled, abandoned outside the margins of even the marginalized, and I breathe, wake, and sleep in poetry for years and never even notice that the world is changing beyond my window.

To this note, I add for those I've offended and rejected in my ebullient arrogance, for the times I've gone too far in antisocial behavior, being a badass, for the times when I no longer cared what happened to me, forgive me for not being strong enough to be who you expected.

Poetry, in the deepest sense of its mission, is a calling, and is about repentance: you repent because you've been chosen to carry the sacred torch to the pyramid altar top and there rip your heart out and the crazy thing is that inside yourself the whole time you are smiling and laughing.

What kind of nut would do that? A homeless, familyless child of the muse and so I wish to thank the muse, or as we Chicanos call that magical phenomenon that lifts a person's spirit into an elevated sphere of sublime and blinding life-love, *corazón,* where you are entranced and beyond this world and reality, where you witness for an eternal moment an unspeakable beauty you've never even imagined, beauty in your life and in all others and that's why, in my gratitude, I wish to thank those who live in service to others, because they are aware of that beauty more than the rest of us.

Thank you.

Preface

LOTS HAS CHANGED SINCE I WROTE MY COLLECTION OF ESSAYS *Working in the Dark* in 1994, and in the following essays I'll share with you the changes in perspective, spiritual shifts, life now, literary and personal. My journey has more ups and downs, successes and failures, certainties and doubts, false starts and headstrong triumphs, than a Wall Street broker's prediction sitting at a bar getting drunk.

But the presence that underlies these pages is an unwavering optimism that one day I'll get the basics right, like how to take better care of myself, quit eating all that great greasy (yummy) food and drinking too much, and taking my spiritual practice more seriously.

I've been writing poetry a long time, fifty years, give or take a few, and I've never belonged to any literary school, never suffered from the herding mentality that has you a card-carrying member of a literary gang where you amble down the polished marble hallways of elite academic schools, where you learn to use your power against others, parade your privilege, and dominate. The only society, if you wish to call it that, I ever belonged to was my family. Never a believer in capitalism (no amount of money could ever measure up to the value of a good poem). Rarely part of a movement—no trend, no fashion fox, and I've never had an interest in proving myself a better writer than the next person, never been an issue writer when issues came up only as a popular fad to write about.

Never used my ethnicity or gender in a manner that pits me in an us/against/you clique—for advantage—no, never been one of the social literary birds, and not because I feel I'm better or above others, although I'll admit,

I detest pretension for the sake of winning approval; the tax that it takes to be constantly on call is too much. The desire to increase your stature or gain some entitlement that comes from flattery is not worth it.

I'll admit it was a much different world back in 1994 when *Working in the Dark* was published. Since I wrote those essays people feel more comfortable airing their grievances and hatred of each other. I think it boils down to some wanting everything their way, spoiled brats, and others wanting their fair share. Though I don't watch TV, I see clips of those rabid Fox commentators, and they seem like a bunch of whacked-out freaks in a trench holding out to the last man, screaming for more entitlement and more privilege, using every last bullet to try and kill every constitutional right of common citizens. It won't work, you can see it in their desperate eyes, hear it in their shrieking voices—their greed and racism is done. Se acabó, my grandma would say, se acabó, it is finished.

For the most part, we generally get along okay, Latinos, blacks, Asians, and whites, but there are always those who love to incite separations and divisions and create chaos and enmity among us. The hate-media carry those few voices and make it sound like they're everywhere when it's only a few madmen, screaming for white privilege, usually white powerful billionaires who own the airwaves. But I find that, talking to my neighbors, we all generally get along.

In 1994, when I wrote the essays in *Working in the Dark,* I hinted at racism, at gentrification, at ethnic pride, prison and educational reform, and now those issues are openly debated and discussed nationally as commonplace.

That's good, even though I find myself morose these days, in the midst of a daily barrage of bad news and in the center of all this national resentment and intimidation of white supremacists terrorizing and traumatizing us Latino citizens. And I guess more out of desperation, out of needing a break from the minute to minute crises, I find myself in the only refuge I know, writing and reading and being a father and husband.

I've been lucky in all these departments, literary, parenting, social friends who are not so much elites as much as they are just ordinary folks living paycheck to paycheck. They're the best, they work hard, they're fair-minded, they're always ready to serve for a worthy cause, volunteering for bird counts, bosque cleanups, donating a little money for educational start-ups, really decent people. And that's the America I love and know and will fight for.

But this book is also about exclusion, about being left out of the promise that America offers (to whities mostly)—decent education, respect for your ethnicity and history and people, justice, fair education, environmental and wealth equity. Most of these are out of reach to any Chicano you ask, though you would expect that being an ancestor of the first indigenous people of the Southwest, that we, the mestizos, would at least have the crumbs but no, not even that—we are the forgotten ones. The disappeared. And in a great and sad way, due to our colonial oppression, many of us have given up, victims of our own apathy and hopelessness. And when after a long life of daily desperation it just becomes too much, too long without having anything, too long yearning for a justice that never comes, for the good education the kids deserve that never materializes, and one finally gives up, I don't blame them. I feel hurt by what they have to go through, and I feel guilty, partly because I feel that I didn't give enough attention to them.

It seems absolutely absurd that one old white billionaire can have enough money to control national policy by buying off politicians—and through his money direct how our judicial and educational and environmental system runs. He destroys. He captures and imprisons and murders the future of our kids just so he can have more power, more money, more privilege.

When I wrote *Working in the Dark,* in 1994, wrote how I learned so much working in Hollywood, about power and money and influence, how actors are terrified of speaking up, how the industry operates on who you support—Israel? Palestine? How politics of Jewish support and Palestinian support play so much in who is blacklisted and who got the jobs. Go Jewish and you get the job, voice your concerns over Palestinian occupation by Israeli military, you get expelled from Hollywood, marked as one of those who dared to speak against the powerful.

But it's all coming to light now: sexual scandals, the racism and gender inequity, the deplorable white-only roles, and it's a good thing that it's finally coming out in the open.

But change is slow to come; the white billionaire who turns everything he touches into a disease, who destroys with every step, who spews venom on everything he sees—you know him, you see him as owners of golf courses and hotels, owners of hate radio stations and hate newspapers and shareholders in private prisons and political lobbyists for petroleum and pharmaceuticals. He's the Pinche Gringo. Destroyer of worlds, imprisoner of babies, separator of families, wall builder, liar, thief, tax evader, lethal-tongued Tweeter. The Pinche Gringo infects every social system with his greed and lies. (And as I write this, yet another atrocity has been committed at an El Paso Walmart, and if that wasn't enough, ICE agents stormed chicken-processing plants in Mississippi and detained close to 680 human beings, all Mexican or Central Americans. The raid was carried out on the first day of school and the children were left to themselves, without parents, stranded in the streets or hiding out in closets or fields, terrified of the Pinche Gringo lurking about trying to capture them.)

Surprised as I am by the relative success of *Working in the Dark*, which is still in print, I'm covering a lot more poetry and literature and ethnic and justice issues here and to that end, consider that this book is simply about a poet and his quizzical look back at things that have changed or improved or gotten worse.

It's a far cry from a tell-all mea culpa, more of a mischievous look back at the lessons I was lucky enough to learn from personal experience and see from the silly and mean things people do to themselves and each other, what I do to myself, marveling at my journey as I fall short of the 14-karat standards I set for myself, which, time after time, I fail to achieve and retreat into my silence to try again. And therein lies the riddle, my reader, in the inexhaustible attempts to reach what I know is the best in me and never quite able to plant my heart at the summit of that ever-growing mountain.

And even as I write this, just look out the window and you can see evidence of our deception everywhere, the sterilization of our senses, the bleak non-living existence much admired and advertised by publicity agencies, bleating that money is the answer to our woes, to our misery, to our loneliness. Our feeling of inadequacy, bloating our bellies each night before sleep, is not gas but a moral cancer created from our timid acceptance of things as they are and our emotional paralysis to want to do something but not knowing what—I get it, and I'm with you on this, right now, a voice in my head says I should be out there protesting in the streets and fields and prisons and schools, fighting for my children's future, for the right of Mother Earth to be respected, demanding a halt to all that corruption by corporations needlessly gutting our sacred Mother Earth for minerals scientists and engineers turn into weapons of mass destruction.

I think that amongst ourselves we can straighten this mess out. I have met amazing individuals on my journey, committed, sincere, compassionate, smart as the dickens, who solve problems, and there are many of us and if we work together we can do this. But it has to be us, we can't depend on our politicians anymore, we have to take back our democratic power and responsibility for our lives and future and do this. That's what this book is about, unveiling to you who I am, what I struggle with daily, what I dream, what are my hopes, and you'll see, what joins us together is far more stronger and relevant than what divides us.

I admit, in the period of time between my last book of essays and this one, I have become the unwitting dunce of a sit-com of errors in my even crazier and painful fall from grace. While some recover, others, in their self-appointed acclaim go on to transform into hideous creatures, bloated with resentful rancor. And I will share a few of those with you (after all, which of us, from time to time, doesn't enjoy a little scandal), but on the whole, though, I tell you, poets are the most creative, imaginative, amazing, and generous people on the earth, and what we don't need at this point in our struggle to develop democracy toward a kinder and fairer system for all is the parade of look-alikes all jabbering away with cultural soundbites intended to distract rather than inform.

We need unique individuals unafraid of engaging their civic duty, civil disobedience, those who will not blindly obey the masters of trend, the monarchs of capitalism, the dictators of fashion. Take a cue from Woodstock, dress as you wish, sleep in a bag on earth and listen to the music from the stars, create a gathering of half a million people in your heart and join hands with them and move forward with your vision, half-million-strong vision, black, brown, white, Asian, we move forward to change this country into what we want, not what the One Percent try to force down our throats.

That's what this book is about.

That is, as long as I don't get stuck being crowned social media's "best" and the literati's "king of fiction" or culturally "the new Diego Rivera," and trip over all my trophies and piles of money. Because once that happens,

I'm forced to do a makeover, cover the wizard's mole on my nose, for being chosen The Best, I somehow lose my humanity and become a vain, driven jack-in-the-box toy for booklovers who never read for deep engagement in life but only for a margarita-time laugh or two. Should that happen, I would forget that poetry and literature can change lives, mean something, can inspire, confront, and challenge and intrude on a tyrant's and dictator's oppression and break it to smithereens.

Not a day passes where I don't read about some magnificent act a human being performed, be it a journalist who wrote about the cartels and did so with integrity, or about a politician coming clean on his crimes, or a teacher who gives half her pay to buy supplies for her students. Every day many poets I know find themselves reading into the most common things the markings of a treasure and carry us with them until we arrive at the faraway sanctuary where the gold is—that is, where the muse breathes, in all our hearts. That's why so many poets have that harried look about them, as if someone is harassing them, because abundant blessings do that—make you nutty with insomnia and the eagerness of a lover wishing to share that love, as you laugh in the light.

1.
—
The Origin of My Joy

POETRY AND WORKING ON POEMS, this outrageous journey, often disguises itself as a peaceful vocation, an undertaking by the fragile and shy, but in truth, inside the poet his soul grows scales, his tongue spits fire, he develops a personality with an edge from his dislike of people who have no clue what is happening behind his eyes and find their entertainment in TV or their diversion in shopping at the mall. He considers them beneath him, with the disdain of a dragon for a fly on the windowsill. And so with me, I was suffering such grand self-appointment.

So you understand why being alone suits me. Solitude sustains me through bad and good times, a rare nourishment for my soul and mind in today's mega-techno world.

To be a poet, for sure, was no mere academic pursuit but an epic journey, one that lifted me above mere mortals and carried me to arenas with gods and lovers, wine and pleasure, death and life—life lived and welcomed and embraced full throttle, each scar inflicted, a modest grin at death.

The voice of the imprisoned, a soul voice, a heart drumming, sounded louder than the sweet silence of a meditative lotus. I can't explain why, but I've been in a hundred yoga studios and a dozen countries sitting at the feet of spiritual masters, I've lectured at hundreds of universities, given keynotes for dozens of conferences, and on and on and on, and I don't really remember one of them as clearly as I do the razor wire and armed guards when I entered prisons to talk with inmates.

It was almost as if I had been longing for it. As if it held a cure for me, for an indescribable wound that kept throbbing deep in my soul.

Guards with automatic rifles, others sporting weapons in their hip holsters, and suited dignitaries and guards escorting me through the corridors with cell pods on each side and out the back into a courtyard where all the inmates sat in orange jumpsuits looking both ways with bright eyes that hadn't been dulled by drugs. When they saw me, they showed no emotion or curiosity, their faces had that bland appraisal of one looking at a motor and wondering how it works. What are the principles that take it from point a to point b? Explain how you got there.

That's what they wondered about me: how did I write a major motion picture for Hollywood Pictures, how did I have thirty books of poetry, memoirs, short stories, novels, how did I have a family, how did I not come in all drugged out and fucked up and not be in a morgue at that moment, a name and cause of death on some detective's notepad?

They were caught up in my successful appearance, and I don't know if they guessed by instinct that I fought daily not to return to crime and drugs. I don't know if they saw it in my eyes, in my smile, if they sensed it in the way my words were strung together and the softness of them, the doubt and insecurity and pain I never overcame nor the joy I could never understand.

But give them hope, I thought, that's all I can do. And I knew that that was my purpose if there was one, to come and give them hope, even if I didn't have it. I made them feel like we were lifelong friends, like we were familia, vatos locos, and I couldn't let them see my own fear, I had to hide it. And I spoke on the virtues of education and a drug-free life, how one could never hope for a life if drug use was involved, you had to leave drugs, say good-bye to the old life, bid farewell to old acquaintances, change up your whole environment of people and places and habits and things you did for a change and, with God's blessings and a truckload of luck, you might turn that corner where you can again sigh from the climb in exhaustion and see a glimpse from where you stopped, the possibility of a path to your best self.

2.

—

La onda

IT ALWAYS HAPPENS that I get called out by a con looking for me to get real and I do. Midway through my talk at one prison, outside under the security razor wire and guards with guns and dignitaries from city hall and the governor's office, the guards brought in a Chicano convict wrapped in belly and ankle and arms chains, and he sat down right in front of me and stared at me as I was finishing and when I finished, he declared, "How much you getting paid for this? Why bullshit us, you don't give a fuck about us."

That. Was. The Gauntlet . . . he threw down and after admitting that yes they were paying me $10,000 for this visit, I took his challenge but turned back at him: "I'll tell you, I'll come once a week for six months and facilitate a writing workshop here if the warden allows it and if you attend."

Right back at you, vato.

He accepted and now I was committed.

"Expect my brothers and sisters to be slapped in the face every step of the way, to be insulted, prohibited, shamed, turned away, feeling more alone than ever, but those are only initial starting requirements you must endure, the journey has just begun. But do it, the end result is nothing short of the greatest feeling and most amazing blessing you'll ever experience, one you never imagined existed, that you were capable of great human acts of kindness and gratitude and giving.

"You will see yourself open up with the sweet promise of finally being you in the world, the true you, the one inside this prisoner body. From being called a piece of shit dope fiend, you'll, in time, be addressed with respect. Soon, your loneliness will fade as you'll find yourself surrounded with fellowship—friends, people struggling like you, confirming your dream, affirming your work with their belief and commitment. Your days will fill with precious moments."

I decided to film it and recruited Ben and Gabe and Bill and we got to the business of driving up every week. The guys picked me up in Albuquerque around 5 a.m., and I flopped down on the van floor and went right back to sleep and slept until we arrived at Tierra Amarilla. And if the beauty of the surrounding landscape didn't wake me, the brisk chill did—it really is a magical place abundant with wildlife, seems nothing is forced here, everything has a kind of welcoming ease to it, as if it has grown in its own due pace and joy and you were expected, with the cedar asking, What took you so long, *pendejo*?

The jail wasn't like that—it was a jail—miserable and hollow-cored and lacking human endearments. My escort led us through the various turns, pods on both sides holding thirty to forty inmates, mostly in their boxers, aimlessly wandering from bunk to cot and table to table talking and playing cards or reading and writing letters or just sleeping. Prisoners did anywhere from a month to three years, some waiting for sentencing only to return to prison.

When I walked in I saw how orderly the cells were, how clean the halls were, how everything was in its place—that is, except the inmates themselves. They looked forlorn, in despair, depressed, and angry. The ones that didn't, who seemed to enjoy their imprisonment, were lost junkies who took nothing seriously, not even their lives, not their accountability or responsibility for their crimes. To them there was nothing wrong with taking meth, stealing to support your habit, it was the culture.

But the others, they looked sad, in penance and remorse, and I could see they wanted their imprisonment to end. A part of me recoiled at the waste of time and energy and life. At the shame we all lived with. At our false bad-ass demeanor, strutting like we were all about that. Bullshit, we're sensitive human beings who want a life and don't know where to start getting it.

Even though twenty years had passed since I was a convict, I was still a part of them, still feeling like a vato loco, still doing time in my heart.

They could be doing so much with their lives, even outside, helping pick up litter, painting retiree homes, being of service to the community, but no, they were uselessly sinking deeper into the abyss of criminal plans on release, scheming how to get drugs, girlfriends sneaking in money to buy them or drugs to sell. The void that showed itself so darkly and deeply in those pods disgusted me.

We finally got to the room where I was going to give my writing workshop. I stood by the door and greeted the men as they were escorted in by the guards and they took a seat. The room had around fifty steel folding chairs and they quickly filled with orange-suited inmates staring up at me, wondering what I might say and where this was going.

I wanted to tell them we were fucked up for many reasons and that there was nothing about our criminal activity to be proud of—I mean, all we did was fuck up our lives and hurt people who loved us. Not a goddamn thing heroic about that. I wanted to tell them go to school, take care of your girlfriend and your kids, help your mom out, quit being so fucked up. No more bragging about our make-believe lives. No more acting like we're all that and a bucket of goat shit. Time to get real. Tell your drug friends to fuck off. Tell those inclined to keep using, tell those who come over to hang out and get high to stop coming over. Get used to being lonely and mad and angry at yourself for wasting so much life and starting so far back in the recovery race you can't even see the next runner in front of you and all you want to do is get fucked up but you can't because you're in recovery and that means you're fucked, so get used to feeling fucked until you're not. I think they expected me to come at them with a reborn talk, you know, "I saw Jesus one night and he appeared to me" bullshit. Maybe they expected to see me come in defeated, crawling on my knees, dragging myself along the wall, speaking in surrendering terms, saying don't be so strong with your addiction, give it up, be just like a little ant carrying their loads for them and doing the yard work and obeying—fuck that.

Stand up, go to school, be proud of who you are, don't be a measly little coward and abide by the bullshit, but make yourself prepare for your freedom, make sure you don't get used to being right all the time, to being angry all the time, trust, learn to change, learn how to reach out for help and cut out all the gossip and backstabbing, no more rumoring and false jackets, throwing shit on someone when they didn't do nothing wrong except piss you off because they wanted to do their own time and live their own life.

Learn to understand in your heart that you're the one who is fucked up. You did this to yourself, and no matter how many books you read, how many girlfriends you have, how oppressed you think your raza is and was and how messed up our history is, how America took our America away and replaced it with a jail cell, and don't be blaming Pinche Gringos, it's your fault the way your life is, no one else's, and if you ever want to be happy, *carnal*, be fulfilled and have fulfillment, and people who love and respect you, you got to catch the next bus heading for school, heading for the park where you take your kids and play with them, heading to the courts to play basketball, heading to a restaurant to treat your woman to a good dinner, to bed to love her, to the kitchen to wash dishes and mop the floor and start serving up your justice in a kind and loving way. It's time, pendejo, to get real.

I don't think they expected me to be like them, talk their slang, come from where they came from, know their culture and be an intimate part of it and the pain of growing up without parents and in crime from an early age. It made them sit up and pay attention. Not one person was nodding off.

They were interested, and that was a small miracle, considering once drugs grab you, once the petty criminal life pounces on you, the mind hardly finds meaning in anything beyond solving the problem of where it's going to get its next fix.

So I was honest with them and told them the next time someone pulled their chain, don't react. Next time someone calls you out to fight, walk away. Next time you're tempted to act stupid, do the right thing and act smart. Practice being nice, practice preparing yourself to be who you sometimes imagine you can be, don't stoop to the bullshit of calling someone a name, don't do what was done to us: they called us spics, wetbacks, lazy thieves and daughter-stealers, drug fiends, worthless pieces of shit, slaves, sellouts, animals, criminals, now get above all that and start acting and living and behaving like you're not until you're not.

With them sitting in front of me, I talked about my past briefly, touched on my six years in prison and shared how I had taught myself to read and write and then on my release went on to publish books and write movies like *Blood In/Blood Out,* how every step of the way was an arduous learning curve

I thought I could never master, but with a prayer constantly in my heart and faith that I might not decay from drugs and drinking, so accustomed was I to being my own dehumanizer, my own brutalizer, choosing ignorance over wisdom, out-of-control emotion over reason, selfishness over acceptance and sacrifice, I might arrive at a place where I didn't have to be constantly afraid of dying in a police shootout or wreck or overdose. Do not, I repeated, make it out to be like others are conning you and getting over on you, dude. Vato loco, you chose to be ignorant, now choose to be smart and be man enough to pull it off. Cut the shit, vato, cut the shit.

I had a death wish for the longest time, and it stemmed from my fear of living without drugs, living without being high to guard against being vulnerable and open and embracing the world. I was fearful of not being able to cope with the responsibility of measuring up to the image people had of me, of disappointing them, and shaming myself for not being real enough or true enough to myself or having the courage to stand and be real and not be a hypocrite.

I lived in constant hypocrisy because I was too proud to admit I was fucked up and also because I didn't know where to turn or have the humility to do so. I never allowed myself the luxury of being human. I had to be one person on the outside for the public, the person inside me in painful crises from knowing or thinking I was someone else, someone entirely different, someone wounded and offended by life from the first breath—not by any means a hero (as everyone thought), but a man very apt and capable of concealing his pain. And besides, this was the best I could do in a bad situation, because I've never been given to whining and looking for excuses to blame others for my own shortcomings, and there was no one to complain to.

And so I let them lean on me thinking of me as their role model, their mentor, the guy who had figured out the game (ha!). I brought in journals and had them write their stories, mostly about special connections to their grandparents or friends or commemorative ceremonies that played out seasonally like hunting or chopping dead trees for firewood or baptisms, quinceañeras, or hanging out with Grandma, or uncles, and how the family conveyed to them the uniqueness of their culture, that tree in the yard, its cultural significance, and when all the tíos helped build that horno where Grandma roasted her chiles and browned her tortillas, that garden that always came up with the best green chile and squash and garlic, that road or field where Uncle worked or where la familia walked centuries before when they came north with the conquistadores or where their Indio ancestors hunted buffalo riding their horses, stories that keep expanding in our hearts deeper and wider until they reach the height of epic odysseys.

While watching them write, I roamed around the tables. Each man sketched out a rich history, and though they thought of me as their teacher with a broad cultural tapestry to draw from, someone they assumed had treasures heaping with cultural events and relationships, they didn't know that I had nothing, that I was an orphan, no family or outings with uncles or aunties, no home. As I strolled around the tables helping with word spellings, with developing their story, if only they could have known that I desired, more than anything in the world, to have their grandpas, their mothers and fathers, their yards and land grant ties, their history of intermarrying after being captured and made slaves and then traded and exchanged with various tribes for horses, the skirmishes in canyons and plains with Utes and Navajos and Apaches—they had it all, and it brought sadness to my heart that I never had and never would. Sorrow, mixed with happiness, that was who I was and what I had, I had inherited from words. My family was the amazing people in literary foundations and philanthropists, university professors, schoolteachers, hundreds of them had become my family over the decades of my writing poetry. And it was a great blessing. I was a child of the earth, and I belonged to poetry lovers all over the world and though this is who I am, what would I have given to have a mother like every one of them, a father who played catch with me, a sister or brother who loved me, I would have paid any price and suffered any torture to make it true, but it never will be, and even today, as I write this, my eyes water and I choke back tears for what might have been and never will be.

After the first couple of weeks, I had a group of about twenty who were steady and showed up ready to write. They told me who they admired and mimicked, why they dropped out of school, when and why they started using drugs, the stories their grandpa told them, the food Grandma made that kept them alive, and each wrote about his tragedy of being a failed human being and how he had disappointed the very ones that loved him. They described the nightmarish days of being addicts, how drugs had taken their lives and trampled any hope of being able to have a decent livelihood and how their lives were endless nights of gritting teeth and sweating and shaking trying to kick the habit or nodded out and tweaked on meth for days and remembering none of it.

What they had done to themselves or allowed drugs to do to them kept coming up in their work as a dominant theme. The madness. The destruction. The mayhem. The trail of broken hearts. Betrayal. Rage. The gang life. Everything was tangled up in drugs, getting them, using them, fiending for them. Not friendship, not love, not work. Only drugs. And I didn't judge them, I kept on them to write freely and openly, and my only suggestions were on how to improve the story or poem, not whether what they had done was right or wrong—that was their business.

They had spent years deceiving themselves with the conviction that they were useless humans, that they meant nothing, that they were less worthy than cockroaches, that when they saw in their writing a spark of who they were before drugs took over, when they heard themselves as kids and sons free of drugs again walk through their writing and speak, it was an occasion for a big smile and a pat on the chest, they were again feeling human, even forgiving themselves, and promising their time with drugs was over. The writing reintroduced them to forgotten memories, to heirlooms rising from the graves. These writers were recalling scenes and enduring relationships with land they loved so dearly in New Mexico, tied inextricably to their blood. Writing made them happy and inspired them to vow never to use again.

I gave leather-bound journals to the inmates and to the guards and asked the guards to participate in the workshop, writing down a story or poem, and they seemed delighted to be invited and made setting up the chairs and getting the inmates into the writing workshop much easier after that. We were all on the same team. There was no divisive you/them mentality at work here, instead it was us, writing down the stories lived and told to us.

When certain issues came up they got happy, angry, wept, became frustrated, grew quiet, paced the floor, twiddled their fingers on the tabletop, withdrew in pensive attitudes. Abandonment issues, abuse, prison violence, dead friends. Some flew from composed to agitated, others shook their heads as if the memories were too hard to bear and reveal, and gradually over the weeks the lies and self-deception that held them steady in the storm of drug ravages were stripped away word by word and sentence by sentence, slipped away and left them vulnerable and teetering on the verge of tears or uncontrolled emotions. It seemed in many cases that what they were writing about found them at the mercy of accidents, like someone who awakens from a blackout drunk and finds himself in a field, bloody bodies strewn on the asphalt. The cons in this room may have been young and healthy and handsome and happy, but somewhere in their memories they were on their knees weeping with remorse for what they had done to themselves, when some bizarre accident took their loved ones and some situation they couldn't handle occurred, and they turned to drugs to cover up their helplessness, their pain, their fear, and from there it was all a downward spiral, and no one stepped in to help them understand the sorrow of loss or helped them to move ahead. They were on their own.

Now they had their stories and poems. Outside the barred window snow flurries swept across the air and they remembered hunting with their grandpas and uncles. The sounds beyond the window, a rooster crowing or a cow mooing, brought other poems. News of someone's overdose drew forth stories of the good times with them. Seeing kids in the visiting room gave birth to absent father poems.

The weeks ground on, snow melted, rains came, wind shook the trees, leaves budded, fields turned green, and I kept rising weekly at 4 a.m. and slept on the van floor and the film crew drove and we arrived and continued the workshop until the last day when it came time to take our group photo and say good-bye.

A strange feeling of comradeship binds us all together. We've become family. All of them have written intimately about their lives and exposed themselves to me and each other, dreams and nightmares have filled pages of their journals, have affirmed that the writing workshop was the first time something meant enough to them that they didn't have to do drugs—it was important for them to get their stories down. They didn't immediately see the connection, but as the workshop continued, they grew more focused and serious about the work I asked them to do, and they came to every class, saying if not for the class, they'd be doing drugs and because of it they didn't have a need to do them or at least the drugs could wait. The stories and poems were more important.

And every class each student read. And I realized they were not the same men that came in the first day for class, they were different, they looked and acted in a more social and friendly way toward each other. And every class they improved, they listened, they engaged, some cried recalling Christmases and Easters and weddings and births, others smiled and laughed when some wrote about silly shit that happens when you're looking for drugs, and we gradually cohered and developed into a single group with singular interest and mutual respect, and a sort of brotherly affection developed amongst us.

And it was real enough that at the end, when we gathered against the wall to take group photo, we felt like family. Vatos from New Mexico, all united by writing and reading. We were raza, vatos de aquellas, con cora. You can understand, I hope, how powerfully emotive this workshop was.

It's easy to see them as worthless when you read about their crimes in the newspaper, it's easy to rationalize how we should keep them locked up, away from society, let them die in solitude. The mind can reason this, that's why it's easier to move away, get as far away from the problem as you can, write your fiction and poetry, but don't ever come close enough to it to see the faces, meet their eyes, because if you do, the heart will not let you forget, the heart will force you to be a human being again, caring and frightened by what is happening to your brothers and sisters.

(And that's why I wanted to keep coming in—for every university I read at, I drive to the nearest prison or jail or YA facility and read there. Been doing it for thirty-five years now. So I wouldn't forget the faces, nor the smiles, the dark eyes filled with mystery and pain and acceptance and gratitude. I always considered their faces, expressions, my own, for I once sat where they sit, once walked in their shoes, once held a pencil in my hand and wrote my first poem. Dear, dear Lord, never let me forget where I come from, and allow me the blessings of being there, if I can, to reach out, clasp their outstretched hands and pull them with me laughing in the light of day as we emerge from the darkness.)

I want to thank that man who first confronted me.

He nailed me the first morning of my visit saying I was there for practical reasons (if not selfish) and not from a deep commitment to justice. He was partly right, I had bills to pay, six mouths to feed and six bodies to clothe.

I remember he hobbled in on crutches. Aside from waist chains and shackles on ankles and wrists, his face was scabbed and I noticed bruises blemished his arms and as much as I observed this evidence from some cruel encounter, it was his eyes and the sign of intelligence in them that conveyed a deeper, more important appearance of something else.

He was about five foot seven, with that northern New Mexico face, an Indio/Spanish mixed-blood makeup: Spanish almond complexion, alert brown eyes, prominent Plains Indio nose (not sharp-beaked like the English), a mestizo forehead, and high cheeks and strong chin.

I learned when he attended my classes how he got the broken leg and busted hand and bruises and cuts. He was visiting his uncle in the hospital. His uncle was with friends the night before and they were drinking and someone shot him and when he died, his nephew (we'll call him Henry) was so grief stricken, he left the hospital and stepped off the street curb into an oncoming city bus.

He wanted to die and got run over on purpose, and when he told me this story in class, he cried. He cried for his uncle, whom he loved, and he wept, I thought, for himself. For the terrible darkness that fell over all of life after that day. He loved his uncle.

Henry was respected and feared, and when he sat and set his crutches aside and extended his broken leg on a chair, there were always two convicts flanking him: he was a shot-caller. And when he cried after reading his story, after saying how much he adored and cherished his uncle who took him hunting and cutting wood and fishing and played with him as a kid, I noticed the two cons beside him were perplexed, for they had never seen this warrior cry. He gave everyone permission to share.

Everybody wrote—they wrote how their mom found their first drugs in their pants pocket washing laundry, their first foray into the gang world, they wrote rhyme rap glamorizing their gangster life, rap about being true to the streets, about drug deals, absent fathers, abuse, illiteracy and no education, the sweet spot drugs massage in the soul, girlfriends who betrayed them, when they first tried heroin (Española was long the national capital for OD's per capita), and about a long list of dead friends who had OD'ed.

I interviewed them on camera and each told of the power of the class, how they trusted the process and it worked and how they had quit taking heroin during the time the class was going on. They vowed on camera that they felt they could now quit for good. They promised themselves that on release they were returning to school going to get their GED and maybe go to community college and get an education. No pretending or saying things they knew were not sincere. They were going back to their kids and wives and taking care of them. They were going to be great parents and make it this time.

The writing workshop worked in a bigger way than I ever imagined. When it wrapped up, I promised them I'd be back after my book tour and several months later, when I called my assistant from Dallas, I asked her to find as many of them as she could who were free and set them up for interviews with me. I wanted to check on their progress, seeing how each was doing.

She told me that was impossible, and when I asked why, she lapsed into a long silence and then said, "Most are dead, overdosed." I sat in my chair at the airport at my gate in silence, stunned, in deep sorrow. I was devastated by the news, and at that moment renewed my commitment to go back into prisons and work with prisoners, but this time I would have someone waiting for them at the gate when they were released and help walk them through reintegrating back into society.

What little joy they had in this life, I knew, came from our group. I recall their smiles. Their eagerness to read, how even the warden came to sit in on the reading of their work, and how even the guards read.

3.
—
The Darkness

I was leafing through my essays in *Working in the Dark,* and it got me wondering what I meant by that, by the word *dark.* It's so broad, it could mean a million things. The dark heart when it can't express its grief, or the dark moment when someone realizes they've been betrayed by a lover's lie, or a moral dark, or the social dark where white supremacists try to normalize hatred.

And though I often gloss over the deeper meanings, I think it has to do with the emotional landscape in me, that land filled with fire and cliffs and dreams that stalk the landscape, that cloud of remorse, that wave of ocean water reaching over all the barriers and wreaking chaos on what is constructed by human hands, leaving in its wake no marker or direction to lead the journeyer, except the conflicted heart's unsettled yearning for a place to appear at the day's end, where a wanderer can find fulfillment.

But after a few more readings, my search for the essential kernel of what I meant by dark slowly unraveled in my mind like a slow-forming spiral of steam from a geyser that has unseen flames and volcanic rumblings below the surface.

In one instance, darkness meant my being ripped from my cultural roots and left so damaged and bewildered that I don't recognize myself as true heir to a great history of tribes. My existence becomes wretched at best as I try to align my spirit and mind to the incredible task at hand—recovery of my sense of integrity, which entails struggling not only to pay the bills but to fight hard to make sure my children have a better shot at life with more choices and more opportunities to fulfill their potential.

My family didn't have that chance. They were slammed from one side by alcoholism, from the other side by social censure because they were more Indio/Mexican than white. They had everything working against them: no formal schooling, textbooks for those who did go to school, which claimed they were inferior and un-American when in fact they were more American than any white man ever to breathe on this land. So maybe it was this darkness I was referring to.

Another dark was the dark of poverty, of never being able to predict what the next day would bring, never being allowed on the path to material success because they were constantly kept out of all government offerings— they didn't qualify for government loans to help them with feeding the farm animals, no educational grants or bank loans, at every turn they were excluded either by the very people who ran the system and made choices based on bigotry—giving farm loans only to English-speaking whites—or not allowed to vote because their bosses threatened to fire them if they did—or they were excluded from educational options, forcing them into manual labor, because certain administrators didn't allow them to go to school. Straight up denial of their citizen rights.

And they were not immigrants like the pilgrims and pioneers, they had been here for generations living where they had since before memory. They didn't look European. They were mestizos. They sacrificed, they obeyed the laws and still they were never welcomed into the American family, when, ironically, they were the American family. And they opened their door to the outsiders, and the outsiders threw them out of their own homes, took possession of their lands, stole everything they had, and claimed it was legal to do so because they were Mexican Indio. White supremacists invoked the power to take what they wanted using as justifications skin color and religious superiority.

It was the greatest scam in American history, these thieves coming in under the benign and false patriotic label of pioneers when they were nothing more than scavengers and pillagers. Call it like it is. It could have been different. They could have been fairer, more judicial, more respectful, not so savage in their lust for land. It could have marked a moment in time when two people met and treated each other with understanding. A missed opportunity to show their humanity.

My familia, meaning all those Chicanos and mestizos who were here during the invasion, showed courage, tolerance, and generosity. I am proud of them.

When I was born, I came into the results of colonial oppression, hunger, familial violence, and alcoholism. Despite these flaws of character and epidemic emotional diseases, I could still sense even as a young boy their insistence on being decent people, who wouldn't kneel and sell their integrity for money nor steal, lie, cheat. They were honest people.

Maybe what I meant by working in the dark is that my gente rarely spoke; they were a silent bunch. They spoke with the hands at work, what their hands did was a language that spoke about who they were. And if corruption was there, it showed up in the form of bad hands, warped knuckles, swollen fingers. A despair in the hands is the worst to have when you work with them. I've seen fingers filled with despair and darkness, and they are not fat, they're long and knobby and filled with agonies endured in the solitude of one's room.

It may sound odd, but I see the ghosts of my ancestors, often, I hear them, I gaze at them as they walk across the fields or climb up a hill, in spirit form that is, their ghostly presence. Maybe the darkness I referred to was in their self-destruction. Suicide by alcohol. By drugs. By lack of education. By losing their land and seeing no future. Their dreams had been as effectively stripped from them as someone with a shovel beats a snake on the ground and then cuts its head off.

I try to live in a way that makes them proud of me. I try, when I visit a university to lecture or read or keynote a conference, to feel them in me, to see their faces in my heart, sense my grandma and grandpa standing behind me and patting my shoulder and nodding yes, yes you did a good job. We are proud of you son.

And I begin to think that they are with me all the time, and that every day I must cross the great darkness between them and me that separates the living from the dead so that I can speak with them. Maybe the darkness is memory, maybe I excavate it, dig it up like a grave and open the coffin they are in and offer my hand to help them up so they might walk beside me again. Maybe it's that darkness. The darkness of earth covering them, of time, of memory.

Or maybe it's my despair at having no one in this life from that time, from growing up in an orphanage, that I had no power to decide the process of my life and where I might go, and though I fiercely believed that one day my mother and father might come back for me, they never did. They vanished when I was four years old. Life swallowed them up. Maybe that's the darkness, maybe I fight against it because I believe it swallowed them up and they're out there wandering in the darkness looking for me.

Plainly speaking, they became their own worst enemies and turned on each other. If you were too white complexioned, you were teased and called gringo and poked fun at; if you were too brown, then you were too Indio and looked down upon as inferior and uncivilized.

What were the requirements to be given a pass? You had to live in the city, Santa Fe or Albuquerque, work at a government job, send your kids to Catholic school, speak English. Be ashamed of your Chicano culture, claim you were Spanish, be exotic for the tourists who retire to New Mexico and consider themselves natives, who after settling a bit look on us with bemused condescension and private ridicule.

If you elected to be called Chicano and were true to your history, then you elected to defy them, and endured their accusations of being un-American, an outlaw, and that draws their suspicion. If, God forbid, you went to court, then you were judged by a white judge intent on keeping you out of society—his society, that is.

They were making New Mexico white (or so they thought). There were too many browns and reds. They needed to be tamed and civilized, and the best way to do that was to put them behind bars, manufacture some kind of system that would get them there. One surefire method was to look the other way and allow drugs to flow into the barrios and addict them. That was a sure way of destroying any chance they had of making good lives. Let them think drugs helped them when in reality drugs were the real enemy to a good life. Maybe that's the darkness I speak of.

Give them books on your version of who they are and force them to read them until they no longer remember who they are or where they come from. Create a fiction for them that is pleasing and sweet and let them aspire to it, like the nice Mexican with sombrero in hand constantly replying, "Sí señor, sí señor," create that fiction so that they follow it and become your servants.

No, the whites want the jobs, the land, they want it all. And many, many good folks suffered from this. Their thievery was a crime to be sure, but whites called it ambition, called it manifest destiny, called it divine prophecy. And maybe when I was in church as a kid and I looked up at Jesus hanging on the cross and prayed to him, maybe I saw this darkness all around us, maybe I asked Jesus, Why did you let them do this? And maybe that was the darkness I was working in, trying to get myself to believe in God again, a God they created and owned and who did their bidding, who said I should be satisfied with having nothing, with a prison cell, with injustice.

So many times they made me kneel in the pews for hours for disobeying them, so many times I had to stand at the chalkboard with my nose in a circle for talking back, so many times did I find myself in the courtyard while it rained and poured over me because I refused to obey them, would not believe in their version of God. The earth and sun were my gods.

And not once did I ever give in, not once repent or say I'm sorry. Even at six and seven and eight years old, all alone, I stood and bowed before the earth and sun and stars and befriended trees and felt compassion for my friends. On holidays I ran and played and laughed and wondered sadly where my family was, but never once did I ever consider not dreaming that they would come back one day.

So much propaganda they were able to disperse through the newspapers and radios and history books and religious camps. Maybe the darkness I meant was my bitterness. Probably. Put yourself in my place, and think for a moment, how you would feel if some strangers took everything you worked for, called you a foreigner, and then proceeded to dismantle your culture and disgrace your people. I doubt if I'd see you skipping in merriment in a jester's suit with tinkle bells around the plaza while singing an English rhyme to the queen.

I hold those policies and people responsible in great measure for all my people in prison and in poverty and in despair. Those policies from the forties and fifties and onward are responsible for so many youths on drugs. And it could have been avoided. It could have been otherwise, but because my grandpa wrote Mexican on his application forms, because my grandma wrote India on her tax forms, because my uncles had never sat at a desk but spent their lives under the sun in the fields picking crops for the white man, because all their money was pooled together to buy food and pay utility bills, and because they had no health insurance and when they got depressed or sad they drank themselves dead. Booze was their prescription. It was what the doctor ordered, that is, the bartender. In it they could forget for a moment their misery. They could drown all their bitterness in tequila, they could drown the lies they were told that if they worked they would get ahead, they could let go of making sense of the world they suffered in and float in a mindless reverie of alcohol.

Instead of dead kids we could have federal judges, engineers, CEOs, but every opportunity that could have made this a reality was cut out from under them. Terrible things were happening back then to us Chicanos in New Mexico.

We weren't exactly shareholders in the American dream, and much like every other minority in this country we had to claw our way back, and with us we brought some bad habits—we got contaminated as sure as we did by smallpox when the whites handed out diseased blankets and killed millions of us. We gave them a warm place by the fire. They cut our throats while we were sleeping and gave us a grave.

I do not make this up, I didn't invent it, I didn't imagine it. Maybe by working in the dark I meant it's starting to come out in history books written by us, we are now owners of the narrative and we are telling it like it was, what happened, the good and bad. And what you cast as a John Wayne cowboy, we call a murderer. No courage, wolves in sheep's clothing, and instead of Wild West heroes, they were crazy people, fixated on gold, on raping women, on taking what they wanted, making the rules and laws as they needed to benefit themselves and enrich themselves and future generations.

What saved us from extinction? While the whites owned all the manufacturing, we washed our clothes by hand, made tortillas on the stove, and while the Koch brothers scammed and robbed to produce everyday survival items, Hearst and Rockefeller and Kennedy and the Murdochs of the world ran everything, owned the courts and the police, and the darkness, my friend, of which I write, might be the darkness in which everyone lives afraid of speaking truth or acting against these powers.

It might be I mean by "working in the dark" that we are afraid to speak the truth, in fear of being ostracized. Perhaps, I use darkness as a metaphor for a place we're caught in, buffeted by opposing streams of history, caught in the middle with no shelter or refuge. We're always at odds with ourselves, easily persuaded to opt for the easiest way. We've been taught to negate our history and our culture. We need to unearth the jewels of our cultural character and lay down some virtues that make us who we are and celebrate those virtues.

And maybe I use darkness to mean how we train ourselves to believe it's all okay, things are fine, to ignore the injustice, illiteracy, the imprisoned, the homeless, racism; maybe I use darkness as a metaphor for a kind of blindfold. We grope in the unknown, seeking a hand to take ours and lead us out of our confusion. To give the official story, the narrative that will let us believe in heaven and justice and that white supremacists should rule us, that we can't trust our instincts, we need guidance from those authorities who profess to have our best interest at heart but secretly exploit our trust and naivety.

When I was a child darkness triggered my fears and insecurities, and maybe again I have to reach out to that darkness. Maybe I need to trust that working in the dark is when I am at my best, an explorer searching for what was lost, my humanity, strong enough to carry and endure the holes in my soul—our confusion, our fears, our vulnerabilities. We need to embrace each other and purge the colonial sickness that makes us feel inadequate.

Darkness carries within it the seeds of light, an embryonic life waiting to be born, and who knows, who can guess what beauty comes forth from that birthing, what unique and rare bounty it can offer us if only we're courageous enough to take the first step on a journey affirming the preciousness of who we are in our forgiveness of each other.

It makes us citizens of the cosmos, la raza cosmica, with enough room in our spirit and heart to accommodate the stars, at this very moment, being created. I am certain of nothing except that I am the substance where life is nurtured and cared for. I am made of the material that offers a home for all forms of life.

I use darkness as a metaphor I am immersed in, as I learn to navigate and value my experience. Whatever experience that may be, I embrace it.

We need to reconcile ourselves to our greatness, our purpose and meaning, and when we do that, we won't need drugs to numb ourselves, we won't need to fight amongst ourselves to convince each other we are right and they are wrong, we won't need to be divisive, or combative. We have enough empathy to accept differences. We don't need to target and point fingers and make each other feel guilty; we've had enough of that shaming.

We need to let darkness be of service to us. There are a million ways to be you. Pick one that suits you, that allows you the space to tell your story using your life as the epic tale of a hero.

4.
—

Burque Blues

I COULD NEVER IN A MILLION YEARS, say fifteen years ago, imagine how my life might have unfolded. It's miraculous, a walk over the fire and water without burning or drowning.

Time is like one of those tractors that comes out after a blizzard. You can hear the grader with its long blade roaring in the street below your bedroom window, scraping away the flaked blessing, almost like Christmas, almost transporting us back to a time when life held promise of magical outcomes.

But then we wake and dress and come out and find the snow banked high, all curb-dirty and grainy and lumpy, almost gruesome in its brooding imposition.

That is how we experience time. It comes so beautifully, each morning and evening, through school and lovers and jobs, shopping and new acquaintances, everything on initial contact seems to bear good news, pushing us out of our temporary paralysis, giving us hope that when we turn the doorknob of our apartment and go out, something special is going to happen today. And then at the day's end, we lean forward in our coats and trudge down the streets back to our home, gripped by the same despair and hoping that maybe tomorrow will be the day. Our day.

The snow falls the way a good story or poem starts out, one that reminds us of our mothers sitting on our childhood beds and reading to us. But slowly, after she leaves the room, the silence returns and a coldness sets in and chills the windowpanes, the story gets scary, and I find myself thinking, trying not to fall asleep. I part the curtains. The night glistens with a thin layer of ice, my breath frosting the glass. But the stars burn bright and I smile. God, I realize, has left the lights on, and I fall easily into dreaming.

5.

Caught Up!

A LOT HAS CHANGED SINCE THE RODNEY KING DAYS. I remember flying over those riots in South Central and seeing bonfires studding the night, seeing chaos in the street below, wondering if anyone had thought of shooting down our plane. Lots has changed since those days, our society has morphed into an ugly, greedy thing with lines drawn between so many factions you can't even count them anymore. But one phenomenon for sure has reared its ugly head and that's domestic terrorism. Who would have dreamed in their worst nightmare that white supremacists would walk into churches, mosques, elementary schools, high schools, dance clubs, theaters, malls, and peaceful demonstrations, murdering kids and women indiscriminately, and that we'd have a president who tacitly condoned it. The #metoo movement. OxyContin epidemic. Church scandals. Child predators disguised as CEOs. Once unthinkable, all these now seem almost commonplace.

Even some writers, I guess feeling privileged by successful book sales and awards, have turned their once-subtle presentations into grubby, literary mosh pits. There's a lot more cursing. And even the prima donnas get in on the free-for-all: writers who bask in institutional acceptance are on stage cursing and presenting obscene poems to the audience as if they'd grown up in an alley with a bunch of glue sniffers and meth heads.

So many back and forth accusations. Radio talk-show hosts promote a grocery store of hate brands. They'll find someone for you to hate if you listen five minutes. It's like every media platform is a soapbox and preaching opposition as the new religion and cure for meaningless life.

Some even scream in an almost daily blitz, numbing our faculties of discretion and propriety. Our decline in morals and ethics seems to have no limit, we've gotten ugly and evil and uncaring in politics, in sports, in social media. Everybody's become unhinged. Where is it going to end, we wonder, this mass exodus from reason?

I was a boy caught in the wreckage of a family throttled by alcoholism and poverty. But that didn't mean they were bad people. To the contrary, they were so sensitive that tragedy cut them deep. I assume the same is true for these domestic terrorists who seek solutions in bullets not ballots.

There's a big difference between people who learned to work for a living with their hands and those who have shaped lives from reading books, toeing the politically correct lines, viewing life out of office windows, judging a book by how it aligns with their upbringing and expensive education.

A lot of domestic terrorists read only killing and bomb-making books, and a lot of liberals read literary books and pride themselves on their contempt for the other side. Some have too many books, they gave us Hillary; others too few, they gave us Trump; and there is always a reservoir of doubt between the two, leading to mistrust if not hate. Too much of one and not enough of the other leads to an imbalanced diet and affects the heart as well as the mind. Your view of reality gets corkscrewed and our heads spin and spin.

We all knew 45, as I prefer to call him, was the worst thing that anyone could imagine happening to democracy. We know those who voted for him suffer from moral depletion, that beneath their smiles there lurks the cancer of racism and greed. But many of us also knew that Clinton, in her own way, was a guided missile remotely controlled by wealthy liberals. We deserved better and yet we settled for less as we usually do.

We live in an age of settling for less. The rich are too rich to fight against, the government too intractable to budge on our behalf, lawyers mostly corrupt, bankers in lockstep with Wall Street and in the middle of all this, the poor citizen, the worker, trying to make ends meet and seldom doing it.

It's a story that none of us could envision twenty years ago. And when we think back to the good old days, well, they dim, tarnished by this overwhelming accident called reality where we feel wounded but carry on with no external signs of trauma, and yet we know we are hurt deeply, and this wound changes how we view the world and ourselves and others.

We become meaner.

We predicted none of it.

Why?

I think it's because we didn't want to, we preferred betrayal and then we'd have reason to lower ourselves to our lowest standards, preferred to stay in bed and watch movies, we didn't care enough about our constitutional rights and if it meant we could stay in bed an extra hour then let our freedom of speech ebb slowly away. Plenty of us love to argue, we spend so much time on social media arguing our points and insulting each other with our educated opinions, but it's more misplaced narcissistic preening and self-admiration than deeply thought-out solutions.

I guess what I'm trying to say is that when I wrote *Working in the Dark* twenty years ago I was doing the same thing and it's not amounted to much real progress in society or in me. It was all flash and dash. I was a commercial break, selling gypsy pony-ride versions of myself.

And now with this book, I am trying to give you something truer. I'm not caught up, as we say, 'cuz when you're caught up you're not yourself, when you're caught up it means something so overwhelms you that you lose your balance and have no center from which to draw rational answers for your day-to-day problems and wishes. You're lost.

Lots of people I know, writers, poets, screenwriters, actors, are caught up in the heady glamor, in their book numbers, in getting another Netflix series, in what others say, in drugs and sex, latest diet fad, Twitter trend, Oprah advice—caught up.

I'm the same way, sort of, but very different—what I have myself these days is an addiction to joy. Laughing in the light has been my choice of drugs.

It could have gone either way:

I was born into a bad situation, and had to adjust my life the way I used to tune a 327 engine, as I do now the craft of writing. I was born of courage from reading about the lives of great people and learned equally as much by working side by side with men and women who displayed wisdom and patience and endurance in the fields.

Born of a never imagined life, full of discontent and combativeness, squandering opportunities that entailed I sacrifice my honor. Born of inability to compromise and forget or dismiss what they meant to me, even my drunkard uncle and my addict brother, even my father who ruined his life from drinking and my mother who denied her India/Mexican background trying to be white, even my aunts and uncles who drifted along from man to man and woman to woman destroying their interior beauty and grace.

And I was born of those who didn't go the way of the booze or drugs or violence. Sacrifice and modesty and humility gave them grace from which I sprang, those who sought the easy way out, becoming lackeys by getting jobs where they made things or did work that hurt the people, and knowing this, living with this made them Judas people, forced them into servitude doing something they didn't believe in, shaped them into weaklings with worm-spines.

I was born from all that I've been subjected to, all the maladies, moral and physical, born fighting my way out of moral dilemmas by opting for the less lucrative options, making my way through the months and years living the kind of life my heart felt I needed to if I were to claim that I lived my life, not ceding it to others simply so I might have money, a nice house, a bank account, retirement.

Born from knowing it wasn't worth it, to live on my knees was something I couldn't do. I could not kiss ass, no matter how I tried. I could not turn my attention away from the world around me, and that meant I couldn't go into a workplace and do the same thing over and over for a paycheck, a waste of my time that struck me as meaningless.

I was born defiant, following the best of my people's instincts and urges, born from being part of the crew of workers that went out every day and did manual labor, born from knowing that I am the undeserving man who was given a great gift of poetry, born from shame of being an orphan (Yes I have a mother, she's on a business trip [I didn't]; yes my father is coming [he wasn't]; I have a big house [I had none]; yes, I was going to be someone, I had a girlfriend, I was not afraid [all benign lies]), born from coping tactics that salvaged me from the wasteland of despair and feelings of worthlessness, born from the promise of tomorrow, born from having to step aside one too many times, born from never being given a pass, and today I am almost always born daily, recovering and restoring my light and laughing, my friends, laughing in the light. . . . Caught up, baby, caught up.

6.
—

Poet's Prayer

WORLD MADE OF WORDS, words put together to make sense of the world. As a child of five I memorized hymns, singing the loudest in the choir to hear my voice, and at school when the classrooms emptied I spun like a globe on the teacher's desk, touching the sun as if it was a large alphabet card above the blackboard.

Mysteries. I was a wizard and with letter sounds I could conjure spells to chase the devil away, I could make up stories, poems, adventures, tragedies, romances, all at my disposal in my love for sharing wonderful fables the imagination called upon me to convey.

While Grandpa buffed shoes in hotel foyers, I sailed out of the present, imagined a life for each tourist, touched paper roses on tables as one touches a spring petal, scratched my fingernails on wooden staircase railings like a cub sharpening his claws on tree bark, ran my palm along the wall board carvings of Mayans and Aztecas, unwadded napkins on tables to smell lipstick, grabbed crumpled papers in the wastebasket to study handwritten notes, then dashed out into the market.

In time, I memorized the card symbols, fingered letters in the yard dirt, and welcomed the ant and cockroach into my world. I expanded my universe: I traced a letter on the cold window glass and everything about me shifted radically: I was reborn. Words de-created me and gave birth to a new me. I felt myself an alchemist's chalice filled with warm, electric, inventions in flux.

Even now as I write these words, images rise in the mist and slowly unveil what was hidden in the fog. I see my hard-working grandma shaking her finger and scolding me: no writing on everything—in the tortilla flour on the cutting board; in the dough; with my spit beading on the hot woodstove top; when I peed outside in the dirt—"Don't do that!" she cried, "Stop writing letters everywhere!"

Something doesn't work for me in the classroom, drab barracks, portable buildings, books that have nothing to do with my life, test taking and purposeless repetition that numbs the wits, bullying, kids shooting up, smoking drugs from glass pipes behind the gym, gangs—test me why a child cries, why a girl is sad, about a father who doesn't come home, a mother on drugs, about poverty, about fear, give me stories that talk about this, about never having enough to get by, about never being enough of a person to be accepted, racism, betrayals—

I'm done with elitist stories, politically correct, tech-driven testing to make thoughtless and sad consumers, highly educated human-manuals herded together to croon and moo over toxin-laced facts. Testing for me is like being kidnapped, gagged, handcuffed, and thrown into a small cell where I can't move and I can't show you who I am, what I know. I can't get close to you. I can't, in other words, communicate with you.

When I write, my soul unfolds, my heart opens. I look around the world and am saddened and troubled by the maddening violence, wars, quarrels, greed, insane power grabbers, the numbing of America and gargantuan greed of the rich. My parents were alcoholics, they didn't believe in books, they seldom spoke kindly. I like writing because it awakens a new part of myself, one that is stronger than the nonwriting self. I trust the process that changes me, helps me unclasp my tight-clenched fists and exhale and reach out to other hands that help me climb out of my darkness, as I lean toward the window in my soul and inhale the fresh air again, feeling clean, lighter, clearer of mind and heart. It helps keep me from being destroyed by the prison profiteers running the multinational corrections industrial complex that trades in criminalizing and destroying human beings and ruining our communities. May the spirit of my music open my eyes, shape my speech, and give me an amazing life. Amen.

7.
—
Dinner with Alice

MY POET FRIEND ALICE and I sit at the kitchen table and she tells me, "You weren't supposed to be a poet in the eyes of those considered to be experts in literature—meaning White Publishing Experts, mostly trust-funders and country club hillbillies and suburban survivalists. Poetry for them is wrapped up in silk and bowties, like a bottle of perfume, and gives you an almost opiate high in its the-world-is-beautiful intoxication—a literary Quaalude, supposed to have the same effect as OxyContin—take away the suffering of your own meaningless life, or at a minimum, numb you to its purposeless drifting. You do know that some poets sell out so much of themselves they become little pictures on the back of cornflake boxes. You're depressed 'cuz you still believe in the high spirit of poetry."

She's right, of course, the world of publishing is white enough to force one to wear high-tech sunglasses and slather on a bottle of suntan lotion to keep a person of color from going blind from the glare or getting burned from the intense whiteness of the publishing world. It is what it is and she knew it and she wasn't afraid of telling me.

Alice was smart as hell. She went on, "Literature experts, especially the politically correct ones, profess with all good intentions to have your best interest at heart, but those intentions are mere flirtations, and must fit into their narrow view of token literature. In other words, we write under the duress of pleasing our white overseers. No matter how much they deny it, the publishing world is as white as an arctic landscape and any color in that landscape exists bleeding and wounded, dragging itself after having survived the trenches of good intentions."

As critical as I sometimes find myself of the degree world—I mean universities and school in general, where you don't really learn anything as much as deplete your creative impulses and adapt to the needs of society—I had to admit Alice's years of educational attendance seemed to have paid off. She has a doctorate in philosophy and biogenetics (she'd been going to the university for as long as I can remember, twenty years or so).

But, somehow, impossibly, she'd kept her individuality. She's vibrant, original, genuine and compassionate and, listening to her, I often felt I wanted to be like her. She had that kind of spirit.

She went on, "To be honest, Jimmy, you never really made a good poet, the kind the establishment wants anyway—you make people uncomfortable, wary, never sure where you might land, saying too much, saying it the wrong way, too truthful and direct; after all, had most of these mainstream poets not been poets they would have been lobbyists or some sort of custard like that; in short, nurtured on the knee-bowing pretties (I call them), forever walking the high wire of centrism—never too far left or right, never upset the milk-tit givers.

"And you're not supposed to be among them, you're a wolf in poet's clothing or so they believe, but really"—and here she grinned at me—"I know you're a gentle man who is tender, compassionate, even romantic, but I have a feeling you enjoy the outlaw myth that has built up around you."

I agreed with her, especially with what she was about to say. I poured her another shot of blue agave tequila, served her two more tacos. She raised her eyebrows as she bit into one to indicate the tacos were good.

"Some, from the day they wean themselves off the MFA tit, thrive on fear. They find it everywhere, lurking in every verb and adjective and semicolon; the world exists to harm them, rob them of their genius. Their intent murmurs their entitlement, and I'm not sure what they fear about you— maybe they're jealous? You know it's rampant in the literary world, right; really, in my eyes after coming out of prison and the horrible oppression you tolerated most of your life, you simply need a little guiding hand to show you the way though the alligator portals of society. It's not a big mystery, dude— of course you're depressed, who wouldn't be—little kindness would have done the job."

(Just to let the reader know, and before I go on with our discussion, Alice, who is, believe it or not, a Welsh Chicana, bluest eyes you ever saw, golden hair, ample as a peach in ripened spring perfection, is one of my best friends.)

And Alice's right: I have no family, no society, a street kid. First time I sat at a table and ate with a family I was fifteen. Never wore new clothes until I was in my late teens—everything was hand-me-downs collected from Goodwill boxes, shoes worn by others and tossed, never a bed in a room of my own, never a mother, or father, or education.

So to her again:

"But despite this deprivation, you've never been keen on nosing up to the butts of the wealthy, and when it came to the politically powerful, you were worse. Once, remember you told me, an Israeli diplomat wanted to invite you to Israel to read, and you immediately denounced the government as a terrorist gang using American military-grade weapons to murder innocent Palestinian children and women and aging farmers.

"That's why I love you. And I know that there have been some amazing white people in your life who have helped you. But do you know how many poets would have grabbed that invitation? Especially the amount of money they were offering—what'd you tell me, 20g's right?

"Even I would have had to think twice about rejecting their invite, and you said you would too, gladly, if they withdrew their occupying forces and returned the stolen land to the Palestinians. I never laughed so hard as when you showed me their email saying you would never read there as long as you lived.

"They even accused you of being anti-Semitic! Shit, that was a good one, you know, but it's really no surprise, they seem to handle every disagreement by resorting to that kind of hostility and labeling.

"Oh, by the way, did you know Andrea Bocelli has concerts and a foundation in Saudi Arabia—does he think his singing is so sweet it'll drown out the voices of oppressed women and poets in prison there? Isn't that the shit?

"Anyway, always know this, Jimmy, Jews like blacks and Chicanos are humans, none immune from the racist remarks and mean-spirited spite that afflict us."

Okay, Jimmy, your dentist—check.

Doctor—check.

Publisher—check.

Lawyer—check.

All Jews, check.

"So to continue, let's not go into the anti-Semitic rubbish—the Jews I know you love, the military ones bombing children you despise. Means you're healthy and ethical. And you're feeling a little conflicted over the starving children and how everyone here has become meaner and more hostile toward each other ever since that berserk duckling got in the White House. I get it.

"Jimmy, every race has its infestation of ghouls—recently, when I was with Omar and we visited my son's math class for parents' night, a Jew spouted venomous hatred in Omar's face because he thought he was an imam. Can you believe that shit? I wanted to tell him, he hasn't shaved because we can't afford those razors, they're so damn expensive. Also, all Omar ever does is read. Sometimes I'll buy new panties and bra and walk into his study and he won't even notice me.

"Anyway, I wanted to yell at that hateful staring Jew. Yes, his complexion is brown and I love it. How you put him in a box and hate him for it because of the demons that twirl about your head is your problem, brother, yours. You don't pay me to be your therapist and I am not going to take time out from life to sit you down and hold your hand and explain to you who Omar is. I pride myself to be aware and enlightened enough that I don't return the hate, I don't give back the glare—I ignore it as I do the hillbillies and redneck survivalists, who scream on the street at Omar, "Go back to your own goddamn country, dirty Mexican!"

"And they've done this when our kids are with us.

"I didn't know this guy but I wasn't surprised nor did I attack or take recourse in hating him back. In fact, because it was silly—Omar's been so busy writing for weeks he simply didn't keep up with his hygiene and hadn't shaved and his beard grew out and I must admit even to myself, he looked sexy and did look like an imam. A smiling, happy imam, and this Jew snarled and clawed at him with his eyes full of hatred, and I simply reasoned, as I have many times, with hillbillies and survivalists, there's enough hatred and violence in the world, I didn't need to practice or promote it. So forgave them. Call me St. Ines.

"You know, Jimmy, we should be allies, not adversaries. One of my professors, Mr. Durán, claimed that many of you here are descendants of the Spanish pogrom that ousted and exiled Jews from Spain in the Middle Ages. I don't adhere to the premise either way. If so, great, if not, fine. And lest you forget, for the last two hundred years or more, thousands of Chicanos, Mexicans, and our Indio ancestors have been slaughtered. And it's a history that hasn't been written about yet but will one day.

"My advice to get you out of your slump? Just keep writing poetry. Ignore the rabble-rousers. Don't let them get you down, my brother. One thing you know, Jimmy, is that poetry does not abide by suppression of free speech, nor consent to its use for violent or racist purposes. It's a tool of truth and beauty and one need not seek out trendy attire to please the rule makers.

"The reason we're friends and will remain so is that I love you because you've never been a Pleaser—you're a—a—ready for this? A Pissing People Off Poet.

"Since I first heard you read back in the early '80s, you never had the talk or the dress or the mannerisms to hide what you felt. And you're definitely not a predator, one of those who smile and shake hands and wear expensive suits and spout their indigenous ancestry crap and, to keep those book sales royalties rolling in, wail about their subjugation by bullies and declare in the most dramatic on-stage histrionics how they were raped too—no-no—Homey don't play that. Bill Cosby and Weinstein? They're the monsters, not you my friend.

"Listen, Jimmy, you like fat checks and shiny awards as much as the next writer, but there's no way you're going to condone injustice in exchange for keeping your trap shut.

"I know you.

"You're a loud mouth outlaw Buddha/Jesus disciple, criminalized by the American prison system for twenty-five years, too innocent and naive and a dreamer when it came to poetry and what it could do and was meant to do, not well read (then) or traveled (then), never ventured further than the prairie where you grew up with your Mexican Indio grandparents, who never read a book (except the Bible) or went to school.

"You, my friend, were an inferior human being in the literati's eyes, one to be avoided if not excluded. You couldn't get it right, due partly to circumstances and mostly because you didn't want to get it right if it meant live blind and deaf to injustice.

"You remember that story you told me about that Chicana chick from Chicago who came wanting to marry you or some crazy shit? That tells it all, buddy. Tells it all."

I poured Alice more blue agave tequila and restocked her plate with more tacos and guacamole. And as she answered her phone to talk to Omar, I sat there remembering how this famous young author from Chicago flew out to New Mexico to meet me and have a dinner date. She thought we would make a handsome literary couple, wanted us to be boyfriend and girlfriend. I was being published by the most esteemed poetry publishing company in the world, and she had a best-seller book about a girl and her doll or something like that.

Anyway, she came, she sat, she waited, she got nervous, pissed, then vowed to destroy me for my vain indulgence in standing her up. And she left. She then set out to spread as many rumors as she could about me, pretty much all of it hateful insults and blacklisting me as much as she could. I was amazed and saddened. Why would anybody who professed to be a writer with intelligence and sensitivity stoop so low as to spread vile lies and loathsome deprecations to make people distrust me, even going so far as spreading innuendos to people that I was involved in criminal activities and not to be invited for a reading—in fact, someone who should at all cost be excluded from invitations and publishing.

I guess it's true, hell hath no fury like a woman scorned, but I didn't waste a second on it—I live my life my way, not worrying about what people think or don't think. I use my life to live how I want to, full of verve, passion, love, serving and caring for as many as I can.

Still, between the reader and me, I admit I was looking forward to the dinner date and she even hinted that after dinner, to see if we were compatible, she'd offer me a dessert that can only be served in a hotel-room bed.

But as usual, life intervened.

On the drive there, looking all cool in my store-bought pressed shirt and new jeans and Sunday mass shoes, I get a call from Arturo, a vato whose wife just had a baby. The water pipe under the trailer broke, and they had to have water for the infant and themselves. Since I was a plumber once, he asked if I could stop over and help and I said sure.

I didn't see it as a job that would take more than an hour. I could whip it out and be done and go to dinner. Besides Arturo was my carnal, un vato de aquellas, and I did just that, except it took a few hours. It was winter, cold, and I couldn't leave them without water. So I stayed under that damn trailer and got their water running again.

That's the difference, you see—I thought getting running water to this couple with a just-born infant was a little more important than meeting a woman with a best-seller who thought we'd make a great couple. (Wasn't the first time this kind of shit screwed my plans up: it happened with the Naropa Institute once, when I was offered a teaching gig there and I didn't show up for the interview because I had to take a friend of mine home who was in serious pain because he had a piece of iron in his back.)

I may not have gotten a literary girlfriend, but on the other hand I got genuine gratitude and love and the best plate of blue corn enchiladas from my carnal and his familia.

Alice's visit and counseling did make me feel better. Drew me out of my depression. I like to listen to her, as I said. She's brilliant and original; she doesn't mimic others, lie, make stuff up—none of that; but I won't tell her that that night I knelt at my bedside and thanked the Creator. I thank the Creator because so many love my poetry, for all the standing-room crowds, because, though Alice believes everything she says about how people stereotype me, I can thank the thousands of people who have shown me love and respect— whites, blacks, browns, and Asians. All kinds of people have welcomed me in their hearts, that's the mystery and magic of poetry.

8.

—

On a Roll

I was on a roll in 1991 when the feature movie I wrote, *Blood In/Blood Out*, was released. I had already claimed my poetic place in the esteemed list of international poets by publishing four award-winning books of poetry with New Directions, a highly respected poetry house in New York, and now I was rolling out a Hollywood Pictures feature that few could predict would go on to become a global cult film that at this writing (2019) has millions of followers worldwide.

I was living in L.A. in the early nineties, indulging in unending orgiastic parties wherever I went, with a rap sheet and prison time behind me, now a card-carrying union member of the Writers Guild, which enhanced my resourcefulness and made it easier to do what I pleased. I had the consent of society to do so, the richest and most powerful in Hollywood loved me, were curious about me, wanted to hang with me, if only to know enough to predict when I might fizzle out and die from an overdose, or drive off a cliff, or in a shootout with the cops.

The Hollywood steadies keep this machine of love and betrayal moving and alive, huffing and steaming and roaming at all hours of the night and day. Steadies are those who never get out of line. They have hair transplants, facelifts, lip jobs, and knee lifts, that is, they embed kneepads under the skin over their kneecaps because they have to kneel so much to kiss ass.

I carried my outlaw attitude like a Vegas casino owner with a big-boobed blond on his arm. But my attitude was wide and deep as the Pacific. I thought

I was really something—a big shit, strutting my stuff in studio movie lots and cafés and parties like I was chosen to chill at God's right hand and share his stash of coke. While publicly, at least most of the time, I was on good behavior, I made up for it privately, ignoring all decency. You might find me outside in my undies screaming at the crows in the palm trees or swimming naked in the Pacific off the coast of Malibu or drinking a bottle of champagne naked on a hotel balcony overlooking the 405 where I passed out after fucking and drinking all night. Parties with chicks, coke, and whiskey, washing it all down with cash-cash-cash and after all of it kicking back in a chair and watching the sunrise, blowing smoke rings through the golden orb, relaxing for a moment before dressing and heading out to fuck, do coke, and drink more.

I'd come into work with a director and producer high as hell, hung over, dressed in expensive casuals and wearing loafers made in Venezuela, clothes specifically measured for me by a tailor in New Orleans, sporting one of my many Rolex watches. I was pretty much living the life that poor kids fantasized about.

I never even gave it a second thought, never wanted to make it my career, never wanted to live there, never wanted to be good and clean and nice and be one of the movie-lot boys, never be one of the Farmers Market writers networking with producers or Santa Monica crones that wore yoga pants or Parisian suits to work and spent small fortunes on makeup and haircuts and beauty baths and yoga clubs and nails and lotions—fuck that, I thought back then, I was a Comanche, a Chicano Plains mestizo, and you bring a Chicano into your flimsy, white-entitled daddy's-money honey-boys posing as power-broker men and it was my historical legacy to shame your ass, to make you know that I am not you and will never be you, that my balls will never fit into a sewing thimble, that a cellular microscopic cell of my heart carries more core creation and core seeds of genius and genuine love for life than a million white glass hearts lined up pumping clear liquid sizzling like acid vats seething for money, power, more entitlements.

I was your half-time entertainment, a clown who could fall from the high wire in the big tent and survive without a net.

When hearts lack hope and faith and compassion, they dry up like jerky. That is the hollow and empty life of a criminal, and I would never trade my poverty and worry about giving my kids a good education for all your mansions and movie deals and privilege.

I will send you a Hallmark greeting card that encompasses all the get-wells and holiday cheer in two words: Fuck you. When you're young, you're immortal and invulnerable, impenetrable, exist in a bulletproof armor suit, and to feed the tabloids, you go about saving babies from burning cars and puke your guts out later that night behind some cheap red-light district bar.

When I was living and working in Hollywood, it was my duty, my sacred obligation to fuck, drink, coke up, and blow cash on fun and partying. Because who knew when it would ever come again and I didn't want to be one of those who squirreled away his money, invested it, compounded the interest and bought a nice Venice condo on the beach, and took good care of my health—you kidding me? You're young, the world hails you as a genius, you're a poet and you write great movies, you're bound for a glorious life, and the cards would keep coming my way, all up-the-sleeve aces, because I have a gift, not only of gab and the art of bullshit, but of writing. Beyond all the distracting heel-kicking bottle-swigging and snort-choking yeeee-haa-ing parties, poetry was my sacred sanctuary, my altar tabernacle wherein God lived.

I left nothing undone, and once I did it, I'd had enough of the experience of being rich and powerful and knew it wasn't for me and I had to move on and did.

The poem's tribal drumbeat transcended all the flattering quips and ringing phones with offers to write other movies and drowned out the cash register's ka-ching of money pouring into my bank account. I needed the quiet of the prairie hawk in my blood, I needed to sit with a grandma and clean Estancia pinto beans on her kitchen table and help her make tortillas, I needed to hang around the old women and men working in their fields and porches and sheds hammering metal parts and repairing rooftops and digging out acequias. I needed life. Not a false, display window version of life: a picture like the kind little girls used to carefully cut out from magazines and later buy the doll with green stamps. That's all Hollywood really is, the land of green stamps, money, but they all, those writers living high, have redeemed their green stamps for stories they gave away, stories about mom and dad and grandfather and brother, stories they will never recover or retrieve from their dreams long withered on the pile of money they make. But hey, brother and sister, I been there, did that, put it behind me and moved on. It was not for me.

I want to be like those lawn sprinklers that shoot up at sunrise all over L.A. and fill the air with a scent of sweet grass and ignite the air with Fourth of July sparklers and tiny rainbows and birds get excited and kids feel there is hope in the world and women jog on shore paths and cyclists speed by and ex-junkies sit cross-legged on the sand repeating a mantra with closed eyes, while the Pacific Ocean's waves shake healing keys right in front of their faces, saying "Here, I've got the keys to your happiness, here, take these keys, I've got them to the room where your heart can find peace." But the Santa Monica chicks and vegan white trust-funders instead listen to the exhaling waves, never even aware the keys are right there, in front of their face, right there, right there.

L.A., I love you the way a man loves a woman who keeps serving him coffee with salt. Who keeps forgetting to take out the pebbles in the rice you break your teeth on.

I dated different chicks each week, paid the restaurant owners to clear the place and had it all to myself to impress the chick I was with that night, flowers and mariachis, coke and wine, and later fucking all night.

I was thirty when I moved to L.A. to write movies and I went right to the top, my first project a huge feature directed by Taylor Hackford, shot in San Quentin and East L.A., with actors like Benjamin Bratt and Billy Bob Thornton.

I'd had a taste of fame and notoriety before that: before arriving in the sweet caverns of intoxicating obsession, I had gone on poetry book tours and read at dozens of universities, here and abroad, Mexico City and Alaska, keynoted national conferences and writing retreats and gave writing workshops at elite writing colonies only rich people could afford.

Here, I was on a Ferris wheel ride, going around and around, touching ground to pick up checks or chicks and going back up to kiss the stars. When we were shooting in San Quentin (Quilmas, Chicano slang), I was staying in a hotel in the Bay Area with my two young boys, T. & G., and I'd kiss them good-bye and give the lady I'd hired to watch them a stack of bills with instructions to take them out and shop and have fun.

I'd drive to the pier, jump on the ferry, and arrive at my movie-lot trailer and dress out in prison denims, ready to act. I was Gato in the movie. I was on standby for a quick rewrite if needed or a consult with the director when asked, since I knew a bit about prisons, having done six years in Max.

One weekend I stayed in and wrote a whole book of essays, *Working in the Dark*. I had a great editor, a prehistoric rock hammer who crushed my over-the-top verbal meandering, took a metate and turned the kernels of my avid imagination into corn powder, said, "Stop the squalling and squawking for the sake of your indulgent reveries." She smoked, looked harried, unkempt like someone who had won a few rounds in a biker saloon, and I cherished her with my whole heart.

I wrote the whole thing in three days. I always took things over the top, that's the kind of eccentric clown I was, my nature was always to spew more shit on the page than was needed, wanting to be the center of attention, challenging, confrontational, boisterous, impressing anyone foolish enough to listen—and there were plenty of chicks, actors, producers, and agents, and we drank and did coke, self-destructive, teasing death every night and every dawn, blowing kisses to the sunrise, caroused and laughed in bars until the wee hours, so drunk we couldn't drive so we fucked in parking lots, on recycle bins, on concrete lots, in baseball fields, showed up for a greasy-spoon breakfast begrimed and disheveled, gave a who-gives-a fuck wave to worried friends and started all over again.

Anyway, after filming was done, I went home. As I said I'd had enough, even though acting offers came in, other writing assignments, sweet HBO and Showtime deals, and I bowed out. I was married at the time but it didn't mean much. I knew my wife only wanted the money—and when it was rolling in, she was the happiest chirper on the branch. I bought her a new car, clothes, vacation in Italy with her girlfriend, and renovated the farm we bought—dog runs, fruit trees, guest house, land, horse corrals, pastures, the works.

I was a money-mule for her, a disposable innocent street kid making it big. She used me as her bank account and the second my shadow hit the screen door, she pushed me out on another book tour; we needed more money, she said. So out I went, promoting my book of essays, *Working in the Dark*, which, surprisingly, is still in print after all these years.

My publisher in Santa Fe called me to come pick up the first copy, still warm off the press, and I called a friend and we lit out, picked up the book, and to celebrate we went over to the Ore House bar and kicked back a half-dozen tequilas. After we left we stopped off at a grungy Chicano bar in Bernalillo, a town between Santa Fe and Albuquerque. It was night. I convinced the bartender to pull out his private stash, a bottle of mescal, and we drank until it was empty. Outside, I spread my legs and stood in the back of the bar by my Jeep Cherokee and pissed when headlights came around the corner and illuminated the dark. Two cop cars. When the officer asked what I was doing, I turned around and showed him my wanker.

I was arrested and taken to court that night. Apparently, I had had too much to drink. I don't remember going to court that night, but I do recall the unbearable stench of the cell they put me in with a bunch of drunks. After drinking for days, now they had to take a shit and it's in a closed area and God almighty, the stink, whew!

They finally gave me my phone call and I dialed my wife and told her to bail my ass out, bail me out immediately, the beer farts and beer crap and smell was killing me. She said she tried to bail me out but that I had no bail.

What do you mean no bail? They only do that to murderers or if you did something really bad. She said they claimed I spit in the judge's face when he asked me how I pled. Repeatedly. I had to be restrained by deputies. I leaped at the judge and spit at him and tried to crawl over the bench to get to him. Holy shit, I thought, really?

Well, the short end of this is I was forced to remain locked up in that sewer cell for a week until the judge felt like I had learned my lesson, and when I went before him one afternoon, I was more surprised than humbled. I recognized him as the gas station attendant who had filled my tank when we stopped at Bernalillo on our way to Santa Fe. The same guy. Wonders of wonders. He asked how I pled and I said guilty, but not without a smile on my lips. A gas station attendant by night and a judge by day. Clark Kent had nothing on this guy. I pled guilty to spitting at him, guilty to drinking and pissing in the back lot of a bar.

And that's how I celebrated my book release, by being in a jail cell with a bunch of drunks. And the whole time I thought I was, after leaving Hollywood, going up, when in fact I was going down.

9.
—
Ponte truchas (or Getting Real)

I'M NOT SURE WHY BUT THERE'S SOMETHING AWE-INSPIRING about a convict poet, someone who survived the dreaded mercies of the night to come out breathing and be published by the most renowned poetry publishing house in the world and then to go on to make a great gangster movie that turns into a global cult film, then to have other publishers produce another five or ten books while your contemporaries and fellow poets and writers stand by in awe, envy, joy, amazement, shaking their heads wondering when will the adulation cease.

Was my work worthy? I don't know. Was I worthy? Probably not. I came out of prison having published dozens of poems in magazines and poetry journals, with one book published by Louisiana State University Press in Baton Rouge. Shortly after that, New Directions published three in a row, and bought the Louisiana book and reprinted it. Then I got into and out of screenwriting, with a pretty good run at it.

I'm not sure what about me intimidated other poets. My sudden appearance on the scene, that I was an ex-con, that they couldn't figure out how I did it, or that it was a mystery how someone who was homeless, having spent most of his life in institutions, could come out and be so widely welcomed.

They never told me whatever it was, perhaps out of fear, perhaps because the people I hung out with were dangerous bad boys, unafraid vatos locos who smirked at cops, riled up other gangsters just for the fun of it, provoked mayhem wherever they liked—the kind of people never to fuck with. They were not big, or muscled, or rich and powerful, but they could make a giant kneel before them, they could make a powerful man weep for mercy, make a rich man offer his wife for the night. They had that kind of wildness in their blood, the kind you sensed and immediately looked away, and I liked hanging out with them.

I wasn't like them. I liked the women, the drugs, the parties, constantly on the go, another hustle, another scheme to make money, another impromptu gathering of wild crazies hollering and drinking and dancing in an open field long into the night and deep into the day, going to another party, never sleeping, going to Vegas, meeting guys who laundered money, others who sold weapons, others who were lawyers and judges who paid them to carry out a scheme, put people in line, lawyers and judges and cops on the take that I saw with my own eyes sitting around many a table doing lines of coke and caressing mistresses' tits and thighs and asses, unfolding six-inch wads of hundreds to pay for a meal, buy a car, bet on cards—these were oil company lobbyists, car dealership owners, FBI and DEA agents, up-and-coming politicians ready to throw in on any criminal enterprise, detectives, narcs, DAs, and it was normal to them all, the corruption was common, ordinary, door prizes they got for getting to where they were.

I was different and my vatos locos knew it. I was just passing through. They read my poetry. They heard me speak. They came to my readings. And they knew, that with my background, I was good people, invited in to be among them and enjoy the spoils of war. And I did. But they knew I was a hundred dimensions beyond them into another galaxy and they admired that.

Poetry was in their blood. Had been part of their mothers' hopes for them to stay in school, were in the letters their wives wrote them in prison, was quoted to them by fathers and uncles and friends. They knew what poetry was, how it carried the rock blood of deep canyons where million-year-old rivers ran. They knew the owl and the crow and the sparrow and hummingbird were poem feathers. They felt late at night what their hearts pumped in their rib cages when they lay in the dark and wondered when it would be their time, what bullet had their name on it, that the sound of the silence a bullet makes when it's fired and sizzles through the air at their hearts was poetry. Blood poetry, life poetry.

And when I rose to read poetry on stages all over the country, Upper West Side and Lower East Side (Loisida), Seattle, the Quarter, Detroit, Chitown, Mil., L.A., Miami, Tejas, Santa Fe, DC, they were in the crowd and I knew we knew we would leave together and blow the night open.

Some might not be alive at dawn, life was that way, you know, depending on the direction it took, on the sudden turns in the night, on the course the great chef in heaven cooked up for us, it all depended on the spirits, on the laughter and torment each came with to the party.

I didn't know how to explain this to the literary world. They saw me, they saw us, but how could I say I felt more comfortable around these people than with other poets and writers? How could I say that when even I didn't understand it? Except to say with the dark forces of the night I knew I could get fucked up enough to forget my past, to ignore all my disappointments, to laugh in the face of straight people and urinate on the angel's halo.

But I was not one of them, and they knew it. I tried. But it was my kids who saved me. I knew no matter what, I could not leave them without a father, could not abandon them as my parents had me. And I know without a doubt I'd be dead right now if not for them waiting for me back at the house as babies, waiting for daddy to come home safe.

I'd stay out late a lot. I couldn't pay the bills. I didn't know how to be a father. It felt good when I did a line of coke, put me in a forgetful frame of mind, and even better mindset when a chick and I went off, which happened a lot. Coke has that effect on me, makes me so horny I can't abide myself.

See what happens when you take your life serious, you become part of life, not a bystander or spectator. With the vatos I was a bystander, an onlooker, and yes, several times I almost got busted, involved in serious shit where I could have gone back to prison, but I didn't and was careful as I could be. But when I got on stage to read poetry, I was in life, I was life itself. And they knew that.

The homeboys I hung with dressed in silk clothes, had nice houses, new cars, gold neck chains, diamond rings, money to burn, shoes that outshined the Bellagio casino mirrors, and plenty of uncut coke and high-end *mota*. I wore my best, which was a T-shirt and faded jeans and sneakers. I was poor. I struggled to make ends meet, never had enough to even buy myself a new pair of socks.

Some owned fast-food Mexican joints, others were into real estate, some full time in bedding down rich chicks, others guns and drugs. And they knew, like I knew, that their lifespan was as wide as you could spread your fingers but they were willing to play it that way and they did. They died young. They were not mean, they played fair. If they owed they paid, if you owed you paid. They stayed among themselves, they never provoked outsiders or preyed on them, if you were in the game then you were counted as either an opponent or an ally, there was no neutrality in the game.

And when it came to poetry, I took it serious. And I was too dumb and naïve to realize that their lifestyle would affect me, too drawn by the nightlife to know that soon it would affect my life, too stupid to understand that I'd soon be hooked on coke and booze, spending more and more time doing nothing but chasing the high.

And yet, with one leg in the dark underworld of shot-callers and the other leg in the world of poets, I thought I was in control, that I could handle both worlds, merge into one wildly brazen presence that showed the world how bad I was. I could do it, and nothing would affect me in a bad way. I was on top of the world, that's how I walked and talked and lived, despite all evidence to the contrary.

I think they liked me because I gave them social credibility, took them out of their criminal sphere and that menacing aura that clung to them and lit them up in a room as just ordinary people who loved books when they were anything but. They were proud of my having made it out of the gutter of day-to-day life and actually having the balls to write poetry and get published and have my books in bookstores. I was someone special in their eyes. I could speak and articulate and express my feelings and they liked that. I was not in the game, not scheming a hustle, none of that—I was just there to keep them company and party, get fucked up with them.

I'd often pile them in my car and take them with me to readings, or I'd go in their nice rides and they'd always treat me to dinner, always coke, drinks, women. I had special status with them, had done my time, was trying to make my way through the world as a poet, hadn't sold out to their mind and become a punk, talking shit about their lifestyle. They seemed to assume that I knew their hearts.

Years and years of this lifestyle went by with me living this kind of dual life, sometimes feeling like a hypocrite, other times feeling proud, too afraid to leave it for long, too afraid to hurl myself into the literary life headlong and cut all ties to them. I kept yo-yoing back and forth until I realized decades had gone by and I had to take a stance for the straight life, the clean life, the life without duplicity. Saying one thing and doing another had just gone on too long, and little by little they were dying off in OD's, gunfights, prison, diseases like AIDS and heroin addiction, suicides, or simply one day vanishing, never to be heard from again.

There were times in our friendship when I struggled to be like them; handled guns at the table like I knew them, agreed with them when talking about how fucked up someone was, talked up the outlaw life like it was the best, laughed at stupid jokes that made no sense and were absolutely humorless, lied that we were brothers to the end, when in fact, the bottom line was that I enjoyed using them for their free drugs.

They were there when I needed them, when I didn't know what else to do with my life, when I felt a failure and useless and when I was going nowhere. And it was cheaper than therapy or keeping up with the health insurance payments to buy meds.

Eventually, though, I had to admit all this to myself. I knew I tried to keep up appearances, but that was what it was, appearances. I couldn't take the next step and become a criminal, I toyed with the idea, even convinced some of them I was like them. But eventually I had to get real. So many times when I'm on a book tour or giving a writing workshop or get an email asking for advice, I want to say the best thing you can do is get real, but I know, oh how I know, to get to the point where you look in the mirror and stare into your eyes and say, "Get real," takes a long time and it's a long, long road to get there. You have to hurt a lot of people who love you to get there, and then not say you're sorry but start being who they know you are and who they love.

I had to crawl my way out of that darkness, had to pray hard, surround myself with new friends, trust people, open my heart even though I was terrified of being hurt and rejected, which I often was by celebrity poets and rich writers who saw me as too outlawish, too crazy, too criminally inclined, too weird, who were afraid of me, not knowing what to say to me, how to talk, where to begin striking up a friendship. They chose to keep the rumors going, the gossip hot, I was something for them to talk about for the next twenty years, because I interested them that much. I think they wished they could have been the ones to save me from myself. Even as they went on to important university posts and awards for their work, I knew I was a much more gifted poet, and it was proven in example after example, where they stood embarrassed after the crowds of poetry lovers had come to hear me read. And though the literary establishment had hailed these other poets as great, had fondled them with kid gloves and supported them with grants and fellowships and company acclaim, they sat and listened to me read poetry and, against all their efforts, loved me.

10.

The Poets We Need

I WAS NEVER TRAINED IN THE TRADITIONAL SENSE TO BE A POET—no creative writing classes, no poetry classes, no writing colonies, no writers' retreats, and although I wish I had had some of those experiences, I'm as much a part of the literati as the Chicano chile grower in the South Valley.

And you can probably tell as much with a cursory glance at my desk, I mean, my office if that's what you want to call it, stretching the meaning of the term. It's actually my bedroom, has a big fireplace, wood floor, French doors facing west, two windows, one north the other south. My desk is cluttered—a modest wooden table with no drawers, something you can pick up easily at a yard sale for two bucks. To the left is a stack of books I've finished reading and keep handy to revisit certain passages I highlighted, sleight-of-hand literary techniques and stylistic aerial maneuvers, a box of tissue, letters from prisoners I want to reply to but haven't had time, some are months old, other letters from publishers and editors, more books, unread, a notepad for jotting down ideas quickly, three various containers stuffed with pens, Sharpies, yellow highlighters, a sprinkler head with directions for spray-adjustment, a Rubik's cube I've never had the guts to try, and sitting on top of it a small dark statue of Lord Ganesh, a stack of folders with work I'm going to get to, a palm-sized ceramic bowl with eyeglass cloth I use to clean my reading spectacles, eyeglasses for distance, coffee cup, shirt-pocket notebook—on the whole, an assemblage of pretty much useless debris that to the uninformed observer would best be swept into the trash can.

I agree. I have a portable wardrobe in one corner, in the other a bookshelf and milk crates with more folders of screenplays and outlines of stories and novels and poems I've got to get to, then my bed, one of those memory-foam getups I wish I hadn't bought, with no frame or headboard, and to my right behind me a printer, and opposite it another bureau for my underwear and socks and more personal knickknacks.

It doesn't even come close to the office you see in movies where you walk in and there's this magnificent cherrywood library of books and beautiful desk and lamps.

I've often visited professors' offices. They're okay. Nothing fancy, nothing too comforting, and that surprises me because they've given their entire lives over to wanting to write poetry or novels and they've racked up gruesome debt, plus the cost to their personal lives. Many have had serious crashes occur in their lives because they wanted to write and here they find themselves in the ugly comfort zone, teaching to pay bills and their passion to be a poet relegated to a part-time hobby that seems to drift farther and farther away like a sailboat you see when you are sitting on the beach drinking your misery away with a bottle of tequila.

I've had a bad time surviving but I've never made what I love my hobby. I couldn't; I didn't have it in me to say, "Okay, I'll take this teaching position and write on the side." I ain't got that kind of time. And I agree, to get over the constant humps and downright earthquakes that come up on you when it's time to pay the bills, get your kids school clothes, sign them for summer swimming, buy them laptops, iPhones, nice clothes, school supplies, and then on top of that to be married to a woman who loves shopping, getting nails and hair for two hundred bucks, more clothes, and who came to you with no dowry, a poor goatherding woman who had an ass you couldn't resist and a face like a Mexican Madonna, and you fell for her for the whole package and surrendered your intelligence and logic and reason and became a babbling buffoon for the next thirty years because you can't get enough of her ass and lips and love, all of this, no matter how you lay the numbers down, no math has ever been discovered to answer your madness, your absolutely insane blessing for having a life as a poet.

But you do, and you love it, it's a place with no comfort zones, everywhere you step your feet get burned, you're shot with arrows of demeaning comments, you can never catch up on the bills, never have enough for anything that comes up day to day, but you keep writing poetry like some madman who has gone past being able to be saved or redeemed. People hate you, love you, avoid you, envy you for being a poet.

And no one knows your life. It's as mysterious as agents and publishers are, you never know why they say no, or yes, or why one loves your new manuscript and the other hates it. They're young, unexperienced editors, live in cramped lofts for high rent, and you can bet your whole penny jar they don't have a clue what Chicano culture is, don't know what medicine resides in a prairie blossom or have never three-stepped in a tribal dance on the prairie.

So you're screwed from every angle and that in itself deserves a prize but all you get is more a slap in the mug. Go look for pity on the men's urinal wall where losers inscribe philosophical phrases hoping a drunken stranger will read it and make their opinion important for a second. All of life seems to be a store parking lot or a doorstep of a private residence and the owners come out constantly chasing you off, screaming, "You're trespassing!"

You're a poacher—you take what you can from here and there, eat fruit, get drunk too often, indulge in cocaine too much, bullshit your frustrations away until you sit yourself on the floor and meditate and pray that any god, even the most minuscule and forgotten god, will come out of his mouse hole and please, please, God of Mice, help you write something that is fairly and modestly decent.

And so it goes, if this poet's daily life were a map, the topography of ups and downs would drive even a roller-coaster engineer mad. Nah, it's not worth it—but it is.

I've never accepted those beautiful offers to teach at a university, though I should have and I might one day, but right now the poem calls me from the blue sky, from the tree, and I must respond.

My teachers have been other poets I read. Poetry attracts the strangest people, none weirder than me. Alurista showing up on a Juárez stage with a machine gun because he thought there were assassins in the audience; Ricardo Sánchez, so brilliant a philosopher people fled his readings; the exotic El Tigre, showing up dressed like he had just stepped off an Azteca pyramid after having sacrificed a hundred hearts; Lalo Delgado and Oscar Zeta Acosta, the Brown Buffalo—how these poets and writers pulled their still-beating hearts from their chests and placed them on the page is beyond me. They were never known as prize winners and never ones to step on stage in Oz with Dorothy in her ruby slippers.

My teachers were Tibo J. Chávez, who lectured on desert herbs and how they could heal what ailments, or Cecilio Garcia-Camarillo, with his Buddha quietness and his ever-understanding placid face, and there were so many others who taught me that poetry comes from the blood, from wounds, from trying to get inside the smell of a potato and tell what it smells like, watching Grandma weave, Father at dusk in his quiet moment, none of this pitter-patter stuff that reduces poetry to simply tearoom chat intended to flatter the listener with intellectual references.

Thank god I am one of those still grubbing and fighting for respect, still watching this once-gorgeous flower turn stale and wither before me, and she gets meaner by the day and I love her all the more because I understand what she's feeling and I write my heart out trying to put her aging beauty in a poem. I want the wounds, not the willowy upper-class moochers, I want the eccentrics, the ones who are still trying to prove to themselves they can write a poem because it trails them everywhere, not the sound-bite poets, not the botanist poet who pins the butterfly's wings down and encloses it in a glass case to show her visitors. I want the kid coming in who says I've traveled a thousand miles to show you this poem, someone who has no patience for small talk, who is a loner, who makes a fool of himself getting drunk because he's so frustrated by a poem, someone who is feared and reviled by the established literati and regaled by common folks, someone uncivilized, who never gets it right but who stays up late making notes, who's never worn a suit, who has no lawyer look over his contracts, who writes and rewrites and rewrites what is already incredible and if he only knew how amazing the poem is he just threw away, that kind of poet we need now more than ever, not the Italian shoe-wearing showboating bore, all talk and no balls. Give me the poet who paces as if imprisoned in a cell, the poet who smells and smokes and drinks too much, the poet who eats standing up, the poet whose shirt is moist from tears he cried while writing, the poet who makes all the mistakes and shows up to make more, who is always learning to be just a human being trying to catch up with the beauty that swirls all around him.

And to that end, I bow to those who came before me and taught me what true poetry is and how real poets live and struggle and love and cry and hurt.

Such poets were Amiri Baraka, Miguel Algarín, the Puerto Rican brother Lucky Cien Fuegos, the emotional fuckups whose worldview extends to homely concerns like when can I buy my kid new sneakers, when will I be able to afford health insurance, the ones you never see because they're always flying late at night into a snowstorm in Buffalo, New York, or the ones who rage, who grunt and weep on stage because the world and their passion merge into heartfelt prayers to any god listening, to any human who cares to offer their empathy, and this has little to do with education and everything to do with being a man or woman living in the world.

Do away with the privileged class of poets, with the wealthy geniuses purportedly writing poetry when it's simply another rehashed version of what their benefactors want to hear. They keep the status quo conventional and unchanging instead of taking a flamethrower and burning it down. Get those who write poetry as a hobby while they teach and slumber in the comfort zone of weekly checks and healthy insurance and paid bills, get them out of poetry and it'll be like lancing a boil, like an enema, cleansing the whole literary body so that we reclaim our right to beauty and humility and decency. Poetry deserves it.

We need to get more of our books banned, we need to rile up the racists so when we meet them they have to have neck chains to restrain them from biting us, we need to get those middle-of-winter poems cozied up by the fire and throw them out naked into the frigid forest where they feel their skin and bones and teeth again. We need to write for those women of color who suffer atrocious injustices daily, we need to write poems that shake up students, make them stand on desks and break out in rap, we need poems to come at you like a snowstorm so you can't move, we need poems that make life unbearable, that treat us to our ugliness, that qualify us as people who deserve respect and dignity and never get it, we need to stop being nice for flattery's sake and be genuinely in love with our commonness.

We need to confront the Pinche Gringos (white, rich, powerful males destroying this country) with our poems of truth, we need to reach out with our poems and include everyone, we need to walk into every library in

America and start throwing out every poetry book that hails the white male as savior—pile them up at the courthouse steps and tell people they don't have to buy toilet paper for a year; this is what you need to change, remove them from our children's classrooms, and replace them with poetry that loves us and admires our culture and that is bilingual, biracial. We need poetry that confronts superintendents who don't order our books, we need the type of poetry that every high school curriculum and library shelf can be happy about, we've had enough poetry that schmoozes like a candidate running for office, we need confrontational poetry that is filled with truth and love, we need to stop subscribing to the delusion of how they see who a poet is and who they expect a poet to be and be the poets we need to be for our youth, those being beat by police and targeted by white nationalists and racists, celebrate the artistic dissenter, the cultural escapee, a delirious captive of the heart. We need to be the kind of poets reading at a Mother's Day gathering, everyone is talking yadda yadda yadda and there you are up on stage trying to read a Mother's Day poem when you say, Fuck it, they have no respect for poetry, and you look at the large audience sitting around in a horseshoe gabbing away with each other and you scream into the mic, Motherfuckers!

And you get their attention and the air for miles around is gagged like a prisoner in a black site torture prison. Goes quiet, blindfolded air, hand-tied-behind-its-back air, air that has been waterboarded and wants no more, is willing to give its full attention.

And the air then turns cold and heavy as if a chunk of ice had suddenly crumbled off the crusted edge of the larger iceberg and floated above you. Everyone looks up, you're about to get rushed. They all turn to look at you with an expression of disbelief and anger. You feel like a dirty runaway in a loincloth who just happened to stumble into a slave-trader camp, tied with a rope to the horse of some adventurer.

Then men start making their way through the crowd toward you, there's lynching on their mind and murder in their hearts (now that's the kind of poetry we need!). Inquisition time, or in modern lingo, they are gonna beat your ass for disrespecting their grandparents, parents, and kids. They have *I'm gonna fuck you up* in their eyes.

And you turn to your wife holding your infant and say, "Go get the car, quick, pull it up behind the stage," giving her the look we gotta split, mama, and you move fast and your wife pulls up and just as the mob reaches the steps you turn and leap off the back of the stage into the car and speed off, leaving behind a riled pack salivating for blood.

Ah, such are the poets we need, laughing in the light.

11.

Reading, Writing, and Chicanismo

THE TERM CHICANO, FOR ME AT LEAST, was born in the late fifties and early sixties. It arose from cultural abuse, educational neglect, racism, and transformed to a banner of pride we could all get behind, rising like an eagle from the Chicano Movimiento spreading its wings in all directions and filling the streets, moving into law firms and medical offices, into the scholarly halls of academia, further into the barrio and fields and streets, prisons and juvey halls, welcoming us in its embrace.

Milpa is the word I think of when I think of Chicano. Milpa is a Huichol word meaning the harvest or place where crops grow, where what sustains is tended and cared for to feed us and our children. Milpa, we are La Raza de Milpa, La Plebe de Maíz y Frijoles y Calabacitas, The People of Corn, Beans, and Squash. This freed us, increased our cultural connections with each other, didn't enslave us in the white man's way of greed nor make us victims of his diseases. We were healthy, family people.

We were. From rape, when the Europeans came and forced themselves on indigenous women, was born the mestizo. I am mestizo by blood, Chicano by spirit and heart, a bilingual, bicultural renaissance vato. As more and more Latino scholars researched and wrote about my history, I read and learned I am connected to the land in a sacred way, that the land was Mother, not something like a car to sell, wreck, use, and sell off, but to honor and protect and pass on to future generations.

I also learned that our political past was replete with Pinche Gringos lynching my people, innocent women and children slaughtered and their farms and homes pillaged and stolen. The Pinche Gringos are again doing their demonic thing. By becoming aware of my political past, that is, understanding what happened that caused us to lose our land and become impoverished, along with my Chicano pride grew my resentment at the criminally insane Pinche Gringo.

The fact that they were proud that they were immune from the law because it protected their criminal behavior really got me. This wasn't the America I knew or wanted to live in. I wished that Pinche Gringo would go back to where he came from, to the places that threw him out, that banned him from returning to his country because he had done the same thing there. He didn't belong in America; he was a foreigner, a newcomer, and should leave.

This was my coming-of-age awareness of myself in the world and it spoke to my confusion and answered my questions. A part of me just couldn't believe that people could behave like savages that way and live with themselves, and another part of me feared the Pinche Gringo and his evil ways, and I needed desperately to share this fear and tell people about it, and also, a part of me wanted to celebrate my people, exclaim and shout to the world how beautiful and giving we were.

The Pinche Gringo's Injustice had already set its ugly cloven hoof in our culture and colonized us, made us believe because we believed the sun was our god, that the earth was our mother, that we were a backward people. That's what they said and stripped us of our customs and seasonal ritual practices that had to do with our farming. It was a religious and political condemnation of us as a people. The white plague spread and brother turned on brother and the young left the villages and pueblos and many even turned against their parents and denied their mestizo heritage.

I needed to express this somehow, or I would go insane with frustration and that's where poetry came in, that's when I started writing in my journals.

I'm loyal to poetry. To a point where I'll stand up anywhere and tell people what I think, how marvelous it is to be me, to be Chicano, and I practice this pride by writing poetry and it gives me more joy than any amount of money or privilege can.

I'll fight for poetry. For fifty years I've urged young kids to write in their journals. I'll tell them that beyond engineering and law and science, poetry is as important to have in their life, an indispensable gift on their hero's journey through life. I tell them they'll find themselves, don't get sidetracked or diverted into easier downhill pursuits that really never fulfill that desire for self-appreciation, keep writing and reading poetry and they'll discover what lies deep inside their soul. Follow that whisper toward poetry, the language of God.

Life in the poet's lane can be pretty wild at times. It's the only life I've really known for the last fifty years and the only one I want. Fist-shaking road rage at my poems, going right through four-way stop signs in my writing, drifting into other lanes from poetry to fiction. I tell you, sometimes you just want to go out and track down people who kill trees and put them in prison for ten years, that's what you feel like sometimes when your writing life doesn't line up, that is the hours pile up and you haven't written a word, you've got so much work and you're not getting it done, all those promises to yourself that you're going to finish the projects and don't, you end up calling old friends to meet you for a beer, or riding around town, feeling like crap because you can't meet the mortgage payment, can't send your kids to a decent school nor afford to pay the monthly utility bills, and there's no place to hide. You gotta go home sometime and meet the old lady.

So you write poetry and it becomes the only thing that equalizes your social neglect and poverty, poetry stands between you and them, guards you against becoming them, one of the psychic/spiritual dead, against becoming a no one.

But still, you try to be a nice guy, treat other poets—people you know can't write poetry—with respect, and see all the acclaim they're getting and you know it's because they are part of the group of kneecappers who thrive on mediocrity, but you say nothing about them who live on their knees, enslaved to their ambitions, hailed as poets because you don't want to get more blacklisted than you already are, because you're not embittered, you're actually quite happy with life, when you know in your heart you can write, that you're good, and you want to get away from them and you'd rather be in a storm at sea, feeling nature, the angry waves slapping you, forcing you down on one knee, whittling away at your endurance and pride until you know you should give up but you don't because to be in the fight is a joy, you must know your limits and use your knowledge accordingly, you know you shouldn't tread where others can't but you do, and you know if you were smart you'd merge into the ho-hum herd when necessary, be humble, accept your fragility, and you will be blessed with longevity, but you don't, you go for it, because your heart calls you to it. Ah, if only.

And lest I forget, you'll need luck. I was lucky, harboring a desire to live my life my way, feeling I have earned my place in the traffic. I survived the storms, which eventually gave way to a calm sea, where I live and breathe to write and read another day.

I must tell you, however, that I was never a deck lizard, lounging about in the sun on a folding chair drinking a martini with other elite members of the boys club who teach poetry. I have never been the kind of man who spends his time planning for retirement, who believes his mission in life is to get by without working hard, who maintains a position of power that allows me to point out who deserves recognition and who doesn't. I am not a self-appointed creature of that foul league of bitter cadaver-eaters who believe in social censure of people with a different skin color or ethnicity.

One of my faults, my children and friends claim, is I give everyone a chance, welcome most people at my door to break bread at my table. And yes, I'll be the first to admit some have robbed me, some have stolen all my tools, returned in the middle of the night to steal my truck, but all in all, the ride has been fun (excluding, of course, those mangy sore-scratching needle-using meth-heads!).

The reason I feel I am so lucky is that I stumbled into poetry, and reading poems, meeting poets, having poet friends has made my life full and refreshing with a vibrant sense that I've leaped full-body into a divine fire whose light illuminated my darkest hours, attended my loneliest nights, and, I know, if not for poetry and books, I'd be dead.

I'm part of a beautiful legacy that stretches back before memory, to those first cave dwellers chanting to the fire and moon, to those hunters who spoke to the bear spirit, to those further back whose lineage recedes to the sparkling cellular matter of star-stuff, to the origins of life—that's where poetry started and I'm heir to that amazing treasure and I never forget it.

The closest thing to the pleasure I derive from poetry, novels, essays, and short stories is the blissful reverie of opiates or accelerants. But literature allows you to live at full gallop each day. Drugs curl you up at the glue factory in a corner and you die a moaning, miserable death.

I've been lucky not to have fallen into that second fate. I pulled away from every hard-drug user, and have enjoyed success in the literary world, more than I expected or dreamed of, perhaps because I don't ask a lot.

I know one thing: if you wish to be a poet get the hell out of the classroom and start living. At least go to the classroom later. You ever hear of a cook that wanted to be a cook by textbook alone without ever actually getting into the kitchen? Going into the fields and planting your own veggies, learning how to grab a sheep and cut its throat right from the flock, lighting the stove, mixing up some spices and grilling it? Classroom poetry is packaged poetry, it's pulling your poems from the frozen food department— stop wasting your time, sure reading is fine, but it doesn't replace living and embracing freedom and facing your fears by living them out and feeling your humanity at its edgiest fragile yearning for God to appear and assist you in your time of need, is the time when you're learning who you are, what kind of person you want to be and struggling up that enormous mountain to get there. The classroom is a stop on a journey where you sit in a first-class seat. Many kids simply don't have it in them to get off and start walking and explore the city and sometimes end up in the worst part of town.

I know lots of kids dream of being poets. They write poetry in school, they read Khalil Gibran, the I Ching, the Book of the Dead, they mimic the habits of suicidal poets, drinking and slugging it out in bars, reciting their favorite poets, even tattooing their favorite phrases and lines on their skin, living in the gutter because it's cool, unwashed, begrimed, smelling of street stench, doing all kinds of drugs and willing to ingest almost anything that guarantees a high, a crazy out-of-mind-and-soul trip, something, anything to take them out of their day-to-day middle-class privilege, where their parents are on standby to help with rent or college.

I think such desires are in the blood of almost every kid, but they outgrow the fantasy, let the rebellious rancor simmer to smoke in the air, and few dare to cross the threshold from this clone-like realm of dinners and movies and parks and dogs to the road that curves into the forest where hell awaits. All of them outgrow it, go on to be stockbrokers, engineers, lawyers, look back with ghastly embarrassment that they were once willing to spread legs to spend a night with a poet, some lost their virginity, others broke up unhappy marriages with hopes being with a poet their lives would improve, not be so sad, many believed they were entering a mysterious sanctum where angels visited the sleepless—one thing we all agree upon, those were amazing times, times we catch ourselves wistfully daydreaming about, and as miserable and wretched as times were back then, it was better than the polished shoes and tie and seven-figure paychecks and office job we have now, better than a wife who doesn't love you and kids who only care about your money.

I'm not a celebrity poet, no merchandise to promote myself, I'm pretty modest when it comes to being ambitious; I'd like a regular situation, to have enough money to pay the utility bills, have a good job, shelter, the basics.

One of the mishaps to being a poet is you create your own schedule, you're your own boss, you do what you want when you want and that ends up meaning you're always doing other things to make the time to write but never actually write because you are sidetracked by chores around the house and stuff that needs to be fixed, invitations to drink, do drugs, party, make love, take care of civic matters and one always surfaces like an alligator in the calm surface of glimmering morning, so you have to contend with the unexpected, continually.

But I guess these are the origins of my poetry, the bloodstream of who I am, that is, the metabolism of the poet's life. If you wish to label me anything, I think an appropriate definition would be an Applied Poet. I applied my poetics to my life.

Walking in the Rio Grande Bosque, encountering the mallards and their babies in the ditches, little behinds twitching behind mother, the egret and blue heron and the feathers from the blue heron I found one day floating in a nest drifting on the current in the ditch, the homeless man's cool camp and his hut made of twigs and branches and brush, the day I took mushrooms and lay down beneath a cottonwood on the bank and listened to the Rio Grande, the evening my girlfriend Stacy danced beneath that same tree, under a full moon, she danced and swirled, her blond hair like a fire in the night, her body so beautiful and strong and firm and young evoking the eternal essence of primal eroticism, and then back in the city to the gang murders and police killing Chicanos, and injustice, and white supremacists rattling their pacifiers for attention, cartels opening tire shops on every corner to wash their money and Asian massage parlors opening up on every block and I wrote, wandering in my own life where each day presented a new topography, a new language to decipher, a new culture to admire—hawk, snake, mouse, or marching alongside thousands in Mexico on the border, not a voyeur poet, not a tourist poet sent there by a foundation or school, no, but heeding the call of everyday people, I moved with them in cars and trucks jammed with barrio kids and mothers and fathers to the front lines where poetry rises in the fires of destruction or peace, where it rises in the doctors without borders, poets for peace, not some new-as-a-gold-piece poet who never spent his energy or efforts on anything outside of academia or parading around as King Poet celebrating his see-how-much-I-mean.

And in the center of all this I continue to be the poet because of those other poets who love me and to whom I owe everything not because they pay me or invite me, but because their work surprises and inspires wonder, and whose poems helped me survive.

To be a real poet is a roll of the dice, buying a lottery ticket and always winning a buck, its folding hand after hand until the other players feel so bad for you they give you back your bus token. It's lonely, you're neglected, you never go out, you can't afford health insurance and most of the time you don't exercise, eat bad food, hang out with unsavory chums who ain't sliding into self-destruction but get a running start and dive in, dying from OD's or shootouts, or rot in prison. These are the twenty-million-dollar poems I get, not the twenty-thousand-dollar deal a publisher advances so I can write nice poems, and compound this with being a street kid, homeless, an ex-con, a Chicano put down by pure-bred government Indians who claim I am not indigenous because I am a mixed-breed Comanche, not a white-bloused got-a-boo-boo with a flower-in-my-hair society smoocher. Every poem of mine washes down the cherished rooms of racists, turns on the firehose of my passion against those who exclude minorities, those who would rather teach whites only, those who don't understand a thing about my culture, I hold their hand and walk them through every moment of what it's like to be me, to be blessed when a red-tailed hawk flies into my cabin and perches on the blue soapstone wood-burning stove, what it's like to see yet another young kid's picture in the paper charged with murder or robbery or larceny or using drugs, these are the ones education missed, respect ignored, family fragmented or nonexistent, these are the ones I write for and about, the missing ones, the disappeared in our society, the ones we dismiss as nonhuman in our hot yoga session, in our Buddha ministries, in our morning exercise aerobics, in our travels, in our mall shopping excursions.

Those Pinche Gringos set on oppressing us with their white-only authors publishing empires are losing ground—word by word, sentence by sentence, page by page, brick by brick, we are crumbling their white castles of gentrified literature.

I have to stay the course and write, be the first to prove a poet can write and survive in this brutal society, in this cruel atmosphere of those who heckle my aspirations and pompously believe surrendering is preferable and more honorable than living and writing and earning your way through life as a poor poet as I do and have done and will continue to do.

The reasons? You don't know how many times, after partying all night at a musician's house, a carver's house, a bunch of us around the table all night doing lines and drinking beer and tequila, listening to music, playing poker, watching a soccer game, laughing and embroidering old stories with new details, imaginative turns and indulging in our fleeting importance, pulling every dramatic fiber and thread from our story to keep our listeners, almost all social outlaws, riveted, then driving home and while they all sleep, to have poetry at the end of my road, to be able to get home and settle in and write a poem.

That was a long time ago, back in my early thirties, but I think what I felt early plays a big role in my decision to write poetry and not branch out into traditional teaching, although, I must confess, I love teaching and I'm good at it. My method is culled from the way I write and what prompts me to write—that is, poetry must be connected to a project, call it Project Poetry. Build a cabin as I did, tune up your car, replace the radiator, talk to your kid, argue with your woman, worry over paying a bill, all projects that engage my life and later turn up in my poetry. It could be called Lived Experience Poetry and that extends even to reading books that inspire me and that later I try to write to, as if the book is a person I address my poem to.

Over fifty years I've taught thousands of students who have written me later on in their careers to share with me how much I influenced them and how without me being in their lives they probably wouldn't have been as successful.

Yes, I know, it must sound like I'm really caught up with myself, but I'm not—I'm just good at teaching and am just repeating what I've been told over the years. Long before it was in style, before poets going into prison or poverty-stricken barrios and ghettos and white-trash slums, became a pretentious social trend, an army of us poets had been doing it, and it wasn't something we wrote books about or articles in literary journals, praising our social activism. It was just ordinary.

But I'll share with you why I did it. Poets are like the cleanup crew, we come in after the mess has been made—a breakup, a disappointment, a sadness, nostalgia, joy, love, we clean it up. We're a full-service trauma and crime-scene gang, and what was chaos we give order, what was misunderstood we give understanding, what was delusion we give reality; this is the magic that draws me in, the magic of reading and how the poems and prose take me out of my present condition and environment and my heart and mind each become a wing that soars above into another place and culture.

I lose connections that moor me to familiar shores and with each word I read or write the sails go up, they catch the wind and I'm off on an adventure, to a foreign place to eavesdrop on other lives, other conflicts and problems and whatever anxiety was biting at me, making me rise and walk and sit and with being conscious of it, whatever was bothering me or distracting me is gone and I am lost, in another man or woman's thoughts and feelings and circumstances.

Could be a bunch of rez kids, elders in the pueblo, raza plebe in ancient New Mexico villages in the fields, students at the University of New Mexico, an Anglo couple in their nineties I meet at the pool for their swim, those spirited white kids in alternative schools in Denver, those Anglos and blacks in Philly at the university, those Puerto Ricans and Nuyoricans in the Lower Eastside, EL.A. homies, the YA in Chino, all those Chicanos in correctional camps, my sisters in prison in Grants, New Mexico, and Mabel Bassett outside of Oklahoma City, my San Quentin brothers, my Attica sisters, all those thousands of workers in factories I have worked with in poetry workshops and those in Las Vegas, New Mexico, at Highlands, universities from Stanford and Berkeley to Yale and NYU, have helped the magic of poetry happen when we were together.

Something happens between the audience and me, some shift in the souls of the listeners that connects to my words, and they know, through passion or instinct that what I'm reading is grounded in real experience and is the organic compost our sorrows and joys arise from and take root. They know that my words touch their tears, take their hand and that we walk side by side down the road of life for that brief moment, unpretentious, facing all perils and embracing our fears together, it's a communal magic that stirs in us and that we sip from the poem's ladle this magic brew that releases our disbelief and our doubt and allows us all to forgive whatever it is that we need to forgive ourselves for and for a brilliant moment—the moment the fly-fisherman snags the trout and it leaps flashing into the air, the moment the woman visits her garden and finds her favorite rose has bloomed—this experience makes us as we are, mystical, alive again on our epic journeys, what we do is purposeful and who we are is familiar and sweet and fragile and we give ourselves that passing and impermanent gift of reeling ourselves in and for a moment resting with ourselves, feeling eternal, feeling all together and part of a community, all drawn and ignited and fused into one, we are all one humanity.

And that's the gift I have. Doesn't matter if you're white or brown or Asian or black, male or female, my readings—my words, my passion for the poem, my heartbeat and mind, all combine into a sunrise where we see the magical become common as bread and the mythical plain as our own breathing, writing the poem, reciting my poems you are with me as one, and the walls and separations and differences and arguments and opposition all float away, and merge into one, both reader and listener, and I think that really is the reason I keep plowing ahead every morning.

When I'm home, I rise at 5:45, have coffee, maybe a cigarette, meditate for a few minutes, maybe read, maybe write a poem or note on something I'm thinking of, then usually return to what I'm writing—poem, novel, essay—and work on this for a few hours, then take off running or swimming or biking twenty miles. Then eat, nap, watch a movie on my laptop, eat with the family, maybe take the dogs for a walk, take a neighborhood stroll with my wife or kids, plan for tomorrow, in bed by ten, and then wake up and do it all over again.

When I travel I rise early, make sure I'm prepared to read or workshop poets and writers, usually find a place to run a few miles, use the hotel gym, eat well, read. In other words, take care of myself. But being out in the world I experience different things than I would at home.

The whiteness of society is annoying. The whiteness of the English language (my Welsh wife agrees with me; she loves to hear many languages), the whiteness of first class, the whiteness of TV commentators babbling from TVs at the airport and Lou Dobbs speaking in tongues about the righteousness of children's concentration camps, the whiteness of briefcases and lawyers and businessmen and their suits and shoes and ties and haircuts all the same, the whiteness of brown people trying to act white, the whiteness of athletic teams from elite schools in their warmups.

To remedy this annoyance, I find a Mexican and speak a little Spanish, I find a radio station on my iPhone and listen to corridos or a bilingual station, I find a seat and read poetry, I block out all the whiteness and become invisible to the resentful stares of midwestern wives, am immune to the redneck wearing a MAGA baseball cap, I smile slightly when I wait in the first-class line, when we land I find a Nigerian or Middle Eastern driver to ride with, at the hotel I find out where the nearest Mexican restaurant is. I make my trip bearable and when I step on stage I usually say a few words in Spanish, I usually read a poem about the oppression along the border, and gradually transform the whiteness into a society filled with us all, Americans of every color and heritage and religious persuasion, I denounce bigotry and lack of education, I read how we must all give the children a shot at a good education and healthcare, how we have to take care of our aging population, I read about prison reform, I discuss drug addiction and the benefits volunteering to teach kids literacy, and this and much more is my self-medicated remedy for the nausea I suffer when yet another white man in power is convicted of corruption, it seems to pervade every level government and the higher in power and wealth you go in government, the more corrupt white men.

Or maybe not, maybe the real reason I love poetry and the life it has given me is because of its culture and the people you meet in that culture: the people I meet in barrios, the farm and factory workers that come from far away to enroll in my writing classes with stories to tell that would otherwise never be written, it's those people from common walks of life that show up with poems and reasons why they want to learn to write that bowl me over and often leave me speechless at people's humility and grace. They don't come for a grade or an award or money, but they've chosen to travel, chosen to volunteer and intern at wildlife sanctuaries that have stories that shake the floor of my heart and make it crack with earthquake force.

I'm not being flattering. I've gotten requests from mothers and fathers and prisoners and addicts and I've read their work and it stuns me with powerful yearning to express simple sentiments and feelings, these are the people that make up the world we live in, the world of heartaches, disappointment, miracles, love, hope, and dreams, and I want my life to be part of that. They come to language after having lived a life, after experiencing life, after seeing the worst of themselves, humbled and glorious in their servitude to others, sacrificing their wages and time so others might get an opportunity they never were given. I love them.

But by turns and twists, I have arrived where I am, waking up each morning feeling tired and groggy and wondering if I can even think my way through the first lines of what I am writing now.

Poets are tough and human, some come to poetry like Herb, a successful millionaire real estate man in his eighties, sitting in his doctor's office when he reads a poem in *Reader's Digest* and decides to join a writing workshop of poetry; or others, after being sentenced to fifty years for crack cocaine, become great poets.

I am so grateful to so many of you for putting up with crap for so long, the many irascible changes I went through, the many times my pride led me to demonstrate my ignorance by talking smack and acting up, violating the terms of decency I want to abide by with people but oftentimes didn't, I want to extend my deepest gratitude to all of you—blacks, browns, whites, Asians, thank you for loving me, for caring for me, when I could and wouldn't or wasn't able to, for if not for you, I wouldn't be here right now writing this.

And perhaps being a Chicano, how we're dismissed worked to my advantage and allowed me to come into my own sense of being a poet on my own terms. I drank, snorted, smoked, because didn't Burroughs, Ginsberg, Kerouac, Hemmingway, Faulkner, Thompson, Fitzgerald and behind them a long line of opium smokers, the romantic poets Coleridge, Byron, and beyond them into the middle ages and further back to the medieval minstrels and peering over them to the time before cutlery, before God, poets got ripped chanting to the lightning, the ox, the buffalo, the grass, tyrants, criminals, gypsies, the gentlest of fragile beings, brilliant geniuses, like them I am deeply flawed, never giving a moment's notice for tomorrow or my longevity. Or what I might look like, what impression I might give. I have avoided a life of guarded wariness, a life of wanting others to perceive you as a success at the expense of never having a life except the ones others wrote for you, directed you in, approved for you, one invented by you, for the purpose of winning people's approval.

For quite a while, *fuck the world* was my private mantra. The card-carrying Indians wouldn't admit we were Indio, the Spanish didn't want us because we had Comanche blood, the blacks didn't want us because they needed to be the superior minority, didn't want to muddy the waters by establishing Chicanos as the majority minority and possibly taking away certain government program monies or having to share the pie. The whites are freaked because they think we're getting smarter and voting and would soon confront them, call them on their inherited handouts. The biggest corporations in the world, the largest poultry and pesticide and shipping and agribusiness corporations in the world in Georgia and Louisiana and Alabama and Mississippi also are the largest takers of welfare money from the government—the secret security paramilitary groups based in those areas are also the largest welfare whores lining up at the DOD backdoor to take billions of dollars in handouts not based on merit but the code of the good old white boy club, and have for generations, welfare bitches in new cars, expensive vacations, their snotty kids in private schools, all of it paid for by Americans who work hard for their money, to be stolen, embezzled, and grafted from our pocket into theirs. Pinche Gringos.

Their corruption is mostly responsible for the decay in our civil rights. They've shown repeatedly that they will do anything and commit any crime in order to ensure the ongoing entitlement they've enjoyed for a century of mostly manipulative politics and secret deals and corporate profiting from drugs and oil.

I sometimes feel we threaten these Pinche Gringos. That the terms *American* and *democracy* and *justice* carry for some people a threat, some wild savagery, a menacing alert that conspiracies aim to hurt the Pinche Gringos.

All of us Americans built your cities, cared for your children, served you out of kindness, tolerated your greed with a sadness in the heart that keeps asking, When will you learn? When? And I think we are very tired of changing your diapers, making your food, treating you like some half-wit incapable of looking after yourself without destroying everything in life because your Pinche Gringo ass needs to have it all. All of you powerful, wealthy white men, we say it's time to grow up, and wonder when it might occur to you to do so.

I live check to check and I've done it forever, lived on the receiving end of people's kindness, even as a kid, if you want to go back that far, boxes of canned goods and used clothing coming in from good-hearted people. I felt blessed.

I've never been a problem-free poet, never written poems that exclude alcoholics, predators, abuse, climate disasters, racism. I am not the kind of poet to infuse my work with a huge shot of Valium guaranteed to put to sleep potential poetry lovers in high school who love it and are fast losing their love for it because textbook poetry is so damn boring.

Sleepy-worded poems vex me, and for young minds strike the fatal blow of death. Why? I believe the reason is that some people still think poems should be about little girls and dolls, little boys and red wagons, anger-free poems, cookie dough poems, designed to appease rather than incite.

My life is held aloft by common miracles in times of crisis, and people respond to that because it's happening in their lives, and often they email me about how my poems have impacted their lives. Prisoners in many countries. Abused women. Rich and poor. I learned in isolation to speak to the silence or my notebook or aloud to the walls. I was the lone actor on a stage no bigger than an 8 × 12 cell, often reciting others' poems or lines aloud. I was pretty content with my anonymity. I was mystified by other poets, didn't know what shaped them nor how they fell into the void of poetry, and I knew we shared certain traits, after all, we loved poetry, for different reasons perhaps but loved words, had a passion for stringing words together, were enchanted by where random combinations of words led us. Walking in the world, poems were my walking stick in the countryside, my ranting stick, and more than on one occasion I have ranted, to a point where I have embarrassed myself and later regretted what I did.

Sometimes the unexpected happens at readings.

Once in New Orleans, when I was there with Amiri Baraka, for the Anne Rice Halloween party she threw every year. Earlier in the evening I was over at this famous short story writer's house just off the Quarter. We were all drinking and I thought I heard him say something racist about blacks, so I reached over the counter we were all standing at and drinking and I knuckle-rapped him one across his nose and he drew a pistol on me. Straight up punk. But, like I said, sometimes the unexpected happens.

With being published and being invited to speak and read at universities, I always felt like I was behind enemy lines because I wasn't supposed to have this gift. Upper-crust fellows were not homeless ex-cons. Even cookie-cutout rookies, mainstream poets that is, enjoyed the luxury of being accepted. Nonetheless, I was happy I had my poetry. I felt like a wildcatter who just struck oil, out there in the middle of nowhere, dancing, heel knocking, covered with black sludge of language spewing up as high as the sky from my heart, feeling like I was the richest man in the world and when I sat to write a poem, it was like putting flame to the oil, and it lit the whole night up.

I had that joy in me of being given an unexpected gift and causing a shitload of trouble with it. Once famous, and somewhat secure in finances, I partied, I fucked, I drank, I never slept, I did drugs. I was still in my early thirties, and who knew how long my good fortune would last. No way was I going to be who they wanted me to be, that is, the establishment, another crayon drawing for their pleasure like many of my contemporaries. I came from poverty, alone, isolated by society, and now that I had the stage, I was going to dance until my heels got blisters. None of this prim and limp-wristed caffeine-free tea, back in the day I was all about barrio brawls and tequila and cocaine and throwing chairs out windows and steaming up places with mad fucking, mad drinking, mad . . . you get the point, it's all about growing up having nothing and now having it all, even for a day, and worried it might go away, that it can't last, so let's do it up the hilt, let's let the night train leave the station into hell's fiery hinterlands and hoo-hoo its thousand love promises and outlaw stories throughout the canyons and mountaintops and across fields, speeding around mountainous curves, hopeful the ride never ends.

But it does.

I had found something that was totally undreamed of and unimagined and it was a joy and I brought that joy to poetry and in my stepping toward my meeting with God on my journey knowing how lucky I was and I was acutely aware that I was communing with God, the divine elements, yes, practicing my craft for academic or scholarly rewards, but also to hear God talk.

I wrote poems about poverty, poor folks, prison, oppression, dashing the lies white historians tried to foist off as truth, the myth of fairness and the America that could do no wrong soured in my mouth like I had taken a bite of meat purpling in its rot.

To America, I was a colorful Taco Bell appetizer, an exotic Spanish confetti fruit they were going to enjoy—after all, subjugation of the nonwhite races really was a game to the slave masters, but more and more people came to hear me and other poets read, questioning the master's sanity and running our poetry lines along the map ridges of the white man's soul and tapping the vein saying herein runs the evil of their racism. For lots of college students I became the main window to reality and their outrage at its injustice, and that made the elite very uneasy.

I invented my own world with words and in my world, no longer sitting at the perpetrator's table in handcuffs and county-jail overalls; I served as defense lawyer, prosecutor, witness, and juryman, and I called this trial to order.

It was wake up time. For me, I guess, even if I was alone in the universe, and so ironic because once I feared and hated books because of the racist opinions they contained, to which I partly attributed to my misery—that is, these so-called histories of America were written by white men who knew nothing about Chicano history or culture and who praised my people's historical oppression by settlers, homesteaders, and pioneers who pretty much came west and pillaged, raped, and lynched my people. These white historians called them heroes and adventurers and frontiersmen, while we feared them and knew them as murderers and thieves.

However, once freed from the literary yoke of American fairy tales dressed up in the costume of legitimate history, once I cut the hangman's rope of mainstream literature that teachers and professors collared us young people of color with, under the duress of failing or passing a class, chastised us into obedience, forcing us to suffer the colonial bigotry, I went beyond established white male literary canons on my own initiative and broke through the boundaries of mainstream American literature and I discovered other books not on the curriculum written by women and men of color—well damn, the whole world lit up and freed me to love and think and live again.

The Lord answered my prayers: as a boy in the orphanage, every night I got on my knees and prayed to the Lord to return my parents, rewind that trauma-tape of abandonment, but years later I find myself on my knees thanking the creator for giving me other parents of all ethnicities, ones I've adopted in the books I've read that filled me with a certain kind of awe of self-acceptance, a sweet power that made me look at the future and savor it with a sense of hope and confidence that I was part of some larger community.

I hate this sense that I see in others where they drudge through the day in a self-appointed martyrdom. Not for me. When I read a book, I feel happy, healthy, notorious even, as if I'm committing something illegal because in reading lies so much power to create oneself, like I could do anything, like I could be anyone, have any life I chose, have it all.

And when I read, I notice my mind gets clearer, I somehow get what other people are talking about, I understand why they get pissed, why they don't like me, why they'd like to shut me up and put me back in a cell—I get it, I understand their rage and hatred of me and what I say.

Now when I'm riding my bicycle and someone (one of Trump's country club hillbillies) yells, "You're taking our jobs away!" or I am accused of wasting my talent by another writer, "Why do you sink into the prison reform crap—that's backwater stuff, write for the general reader, they love you" (meaning the middle-class white reader) or when I say over dinner with other writers around the table that I abhor the Israeli government massacring Palestinian women and children, and one of the guests who is politically passionate spits back, "The Arab throws gays from rooftops, forces women to wear ancient garb, Israel is gay and women friendly. The Arabs who live in Israel probably have more rights than in any Arab country. Many go to the top universities. And there are several Israeli MPs in their parliament. I don't think you can point to a single Muslim country where Jews are allowed even the most basic rights yet no one focuses on this." I smile. I understand. I am empathetic, and I recite from memory a poem from an Arab poet on the value of children and how women all are our mothers and sisters.

Whether they are opposing me or agreeing with me, I've grown to love the fellowship of poets and writers, felt blessed to be surrounded by this ministry across the world who huddle under desk lamps reading and writing in apartments from NYC to L.A. to Chile to Alaska, absorbed in the blissful trade of word crafting.

I don't know how I knew this about my history and the people that shaped it and me, but I knew that they made the rules that benefited only them, Pinche Gringos, who owned the land once ours, and pretty much had rigged the social system to curry to their needs at the cost of all others. So you can understand how odd yet pleasurable it was to find a school district banning seven of my books, sending out extreme right-wing nationalists to empty the desks and shelves of every high school library and classroom of my books. They were now afraid of my words and my ideas as I was once of theirs.

I enjoy discomfiting the censors, those Pinche Gringo white-collar administrators who would be elated if they were allowed to choose who is permitted to write and read.

But while that aspect of slavery is dead and buried, others are not— slavery still persists and is practiced by many employers in the Southwest as witnessed by the armies of field-workers who live in squalid grower's camps, beaten, arrested, and jailed if they complain and deported so growers don't have to pay them. (Not to mention the concentration camps along the border!)

Perhaps there's an evil little imp in some that wishes I hadn't learned to read, like many of the laborers. After all, a number of white nationalists in powerful positions, civic, judicial, and educational, have used my stint in prison as their reason for denying my rights after release.

They often point, for starters, to what I wrote years ago—I stole my first book in the county jail and spent the next few days and nights trying to understand the words. Comprehension was excruciatingly labored, came in bits and pieces, and then when I finally understood what the writer was saying, it felt like an avalanche had loosened all these boulders and rocks opening up a closed passage forward.

A divine stillness descended upon me. For the first time in my life, I walked through my memories, climbed up memories, picked them up in my palm and studied the endless array of colors and shapes and surfaces that previously had been in me but that I had never appreciated.

Since learning how to express myself, I have found refuge in words, they've released in me the hellish compression of this mounting need to understand and write what expands in me to the bursting point in my head. When I have to say something and I can't write it down, it creeps along growing to the verge of exploding; before reading and writing I was merely a bungling fool wobbling in the swirl of maddening streams of experiences and sensations, unable to decipher their meaning, incapable of retrieving a shred of meaning from my experience.

Until the word came along and it came galloping and bucking and rearing and throwing me off so high I still haven't landed.

Back in the days of silence I had no context to place my life in. I didn't know where I stood, had no way to reference myself or compare where I was to others. And therein rose the fertile ground of a very painful naïvety, one that made me feel the world mocked me.

No place to look from, no perspective. It was excruciating. And so began my journey from my first encounter with Wordsworth's language of the common man. Byron. Coleridge. Shelley. That first night in my county jail bunk, with my flashlight on the page under the blankets, changed my life forever and launched me on a whole new adventure in life.

Finally, the joy of reading is that while you're reading of someone's life story taking place at the same time as your story is unfolding in another time and place, it makes you pause and look up in awe at how life happens in a million ways in a million places simultaneously.

And it makes you appreciate the uniqueness of your life all the more and also how you're connected to everyone else, their stories, their dreams, their worries and hopes and sorrows, and shows you how in some mysterious bonding we are all family to each other in a way that—for lack of anything remotely close to it—can be called beautiful.

12.

A Journey of Forgiveness

August 3, 2019, another white supremacist maniac murdered twenty innocent people at an El Paso mall. This nightmare keeps happening and it's mostly by white nationalists, spurred on without a doubt by the racist in office. His vile rhetoric inspires these good-for-nothing murderers. The racist in office—we'll call him 45, since I don't want to contaminate myself even with the sound and can't even bring myself to utter his name it's so toxic and criminal—uses his Twitter feed as a banner to unify the haters to go out and kill innocent people. I'm not the only American asking myself in painful incredulity, How did we get to this place, how did it happen that this imbecile sits in the most powerful chair on earth? We're confused, traumatized, and the only way I think we can neutralize the evil and fight back is to come together as people, teachers and poets, in need of healing and hope.

And that's exactly what I've been doing for a very long time. I think back to one of my memorable gathering and sharing of souls and minds to January 26, 2018, when I was on a plane going to keynote the TCTELA, a Texas teacher's conference in San Antonio, and there I am reclined in my seat ready for takeoff as the last of the passengers were loading when this woman greeted me and said keep up the great work and then a little girl came up behind me and asked if she could take a selfie of us and then another teenager came up and asked if she could also have a pic with me. I had worked with them years before at the school for young unwed mothers.

That encounter (like so many others) was an affirmation for me and made me proud to be who I was and of what I was doing in the world. I was their hero, their mentor, someone they could look up to. Better than all the money in the world. Apparently, the girls' mother was one of those I had worked with to engrain in her a sense of self-esteem and the confidence not to let society put her down or men abuse her. And those girls were tiny in her belly when I was reading poetry and teaching her to write poetry and they heard me from within their dark, wet world, beneath their mother's flesh, in the mesh of bones, forming their little hands and feet and faces and ears, and in that wilderness of creation quickening with wakefulness behind the most perfect eyelids in the universe, their little forming eyes recognized the signs of love in words. And then here on this plane we meet again.

My poetic journey has been eventful, sublime, painful, incredibly packed with meaning and purpose. It's so beautiful sometimes I get to thinking I'm great, imagine me on stage in front of hundreds of teachers in a ballroom, my dreams of long ago come true, to be somebody, even a great somebody, giving hope and faith and love to others, showing them by example how we can change the world, improve education, reform prison, demand justice. . . .

It really gets to you sometimes, thinking you're the best poet in America, the purest disciple of his craft, and you fill your head with all kinds of self-important gibberish, especially after fifty years of being invited on two tours a year, never asking or networking, but a sort of lone stallion, people email you requesting your presence and it sure does caress the ego in you. It did and does me.

And that's why this encounter with these girls, and a million other encounters in various ways, keeps it real for me, is the antidote serum that keeps you immune from thinking you are really so damn important—because in the end, you're not. You're just proud someone is paying you to do what you love and along the way you connect with people in ways that make the world better. In a way that challenges and confronts and triumphs over white supremacists and white nationalists.

These people, and thousands like them I have met over four decades, gave me my life, shot me into being, shaped and split me, each particle of my being searing off into a multiverse epic when they entered my life, where to this day, I find myself exploring from dawn to night this wonderful and amazing spectacle I call my life. It's because of them, my readers, my listeners, those who invite me and trust me and welcome me and allow me to be vulnerable because they are. Allow me to love myself because they love me.

But along with the rewards came the challenges and contradictions. Language works on my mind, changes it with startling new surprises. It is an extraordinary experience to feel myself shaping words and stringing them together and to then have the sentence turn to me with whip-fast snapping burning the surface of my assumption and digging to a deeper layer of what was there, stripping away the appearance I assumed was the final disposition of reality and me in it.

No, there's always new depths, unique levels I found myself descending into, where I gasped with shock at my fears and wept at the revelations revealed to me, as words and sentences and paragraphs unveiled what lay behind my first impressions of the world and people, and how these people always surprised me with their empathy and compassion.

This practice of being a poet in the world led me out of the hinterlands of my private life, where I was no one really, lost and broke and fearful, into the exquisite lands of campuses and theaters and convention centers, private schools, rez schools, alternative schools like the Freedom High School for young mothers, barrio community centers, all grade levels and types of writers' conferences, associated writing programs, and seaside writers' retreats, opened to me vast leagues of new spiritual vistas that reflected to me my own fragile and sensitive existence in the scheme of things.

I felt like my opinions mattered, and I began to give my feelings a concrete structure to apply to my way of living. I found what I liked, what I didn't, what I approved of, what I hated and feared. I felt absolutely drained each time I read and lectured. I was a dream-work in the making, a work to be destroyed and remade the next day, building on it only to have other connections and arrangements of words born of people's love and trust and invitations cut my new structure out from under me, reducing me often from a spiraling pinnacle to a wisp of smoke in the ruins and debris of my idea of who I thought I was. The curtains were swept aside, and the play went on, finding me this actor, that villain, this prophet, the words often feeling like radiant prophetic divinations mutually shared and believed in.

While I thought coming into language was the end result, the final prize, little did I realize that it was only the beginning, that I was only learning how to creep on my knees toward the altar of true expression, a kind that communicates with other human hearts and lives.

And so it went, tunneling deeper into the territory of reading tours, publishing more books, accepting more invites, my breathing arrested with a new fascination for my hands and arms and body, the same limbs I was told as a child were worthless and unwanted; my mind a meteorite sizzling through the darkness of language, to explode with umbrellas of colors as I looked in awe at people's understanding of my work, at their love for my poetry, at this new meaning of me, this new way of creating a community, this metaphor of me that deepens in concentric and unending joy, this way of writing a poem that carried my intent into another heart, another mind, making my life possible, this life with readers.

Words were dreams. Words were flames that lit the temple candles and flickered in my soul, words were the mind's heavy, edible fruits that broke the branches of the imagination. I was becoming the trustee of a legacy that spanned human history from the first cave drawings to the present and I thought I was the best.

That is, when I wasn't getting drunk and doing coke all night, when I wasn't in bed with a strange woman, when I wasn't recovering from the partying, I thought I was the best and I was trying to overcome these emotional failings, these addictions of mine.

After surviving yet another hangover, I reached for a book, always the tonic that awakened my spirit to my role in this world. So many poets, so many novelists. So many philosophers. And I could reach into their minds and hearts as a guest and take a seat at the banquet table and savor their spirits and indulge in their minds' cosmic play. I felt truly blessed and chose with purpose and frustration to be like them, praying for the remedy that might allow me the strength and hope to arrive at a place like them, with a piece of writing that was what I wanted to say to the world, to proclaim my essence and order in this otherwise ruinous and confusing world.

Time and space were insignificant; I could travel through time, anywhere, any time. I could move through walls, over fences, fly in space, visit anyone, be present in the rain forest or urban streets of New York.

Language was the force that allowed me immortality by connecting me to people—people, and their struggles, their never-ending efforts to ply in the worst circumstances a little dignity.

And in my way I try to return that love. I could mention hundreds of people I stayed with over the years, people I ate with, traveled with, who loved me dearly and asked only that I love others in return, the others in prisons and orphanages and jails and foster homes.

I understand the madman who killed so many innocent people at the mall in El Paso (spurred on and incited by our insane leader), his days gutted by loneliness, his self-hatred fathered by 45, who needed him to act out, who would approve of his actions, who whispered in his fitful sleep to do something that would make people take notice. Every racist tweet from 45 was a sign that the killer was needed and should be recognized as a martyr for the white supremacist cause.

And when others like him yell at me, "Hey Mexican go back to your own country, hey spic let me fuck your sister, hey greaser wipe my ass, hey stupid speak English, hey how much does your mother cost to screw, you have a disease, you are dirty," I don't react, I view them as one might a rabid dog chained up in a yard and I'm passing and I want to free the dog from its misery, feed it, let it know it doesn't have to be violent and hateful, that it's a learned behavior borne out of fear and self-protection, that there is room for all of us, even those white supremacists so disappointed with their own lives. When I read a screenwriter's interview in which she said Jews ran the Hollywood studios, I understood her to be telling the truth even though she received death threats. When a friend of mine accused another poet of being a coward for visiting Israel during a time when the Israeli military were murdering children and women, my friend charged her as being an accomplice and nowhere close to being a poet—no poet would ever do that, no matter how much money they offered her, and he said her poetry dripped with the blood of slaughtered Gaza children, I understood their rage and submission. I also understood he was speaking his truth, even though he was censured and blacklisted by publishers for airing what he thought.

My poetry has attracted into my life plenty of Jewish friends who are progressive and aren't afraid of the truth. I also knew that those white nationalists willing to destroy others by going into churches killing worshippers, and others mowing down innocent children in schools, were disturbed, were sick in the soul, and that my job was not to react in rage, but to write from a place where I transcended the hate and understood their spiritual trauma.

I knew war veterans who turned against the warmongers, farmers who tuned against corporate farming, brokers on Wall Street who became goodwill emissaries helping nonprofits to work with climate change and overpopulation and feed the poor and I knew those Jewish women who stood before Israeli tanks and were murdered. Those amazing Jewish women along the border who lay down in the dirt and refused to let the Border Patrol pass. Those Chicanas, most with only high school diplomas, who locked arms and refused to let immigrants get taken. Those Chicanos who go down daily to protest the inhumane treatment of our Central American brothers and sisters. I knew ex-cons who went back in to teach reading and writing, I knew poets who, rather than become the pedigree porcelain poodles of the rich and powerful, would rather pose as tokens of the rich than dirty themselves in the trenches of the illiterate communities working with kids and adults in remedial reading programs. I knew them, knew I wanted to be with poets who lock heart to heart and ply our trade with dignity.

And I have done so, because people, those amazing creatures who breathe and dream and age and die, have taught me so much about forgiveness and that, if anything, is what my poetry is, a redemption of sort for my sins against myself and others, a blessing-lesson on how to forgive.

13.
—

Libraries

I HAVE TO TELL YOU THIS FUNNY STORY about going to court and being charged with the crime of stealing a book from the library. I really didn't steal the thing because to be honest with you books didn't mean that much to me, they didn't fill my world, not even an inch of it. I could care less about books, my world was filled with physical activity, hanging out, playing street ball, cruising in a nice low-rider car with a homie, not books.

If I had money, it sure wasn't going on a book.

I had people, I had the highs, I had the city, there was much to learn from all of it. Why get a book? Besides, buying some coke and wine and hanging out with friends told you as much about any subject as a book might, although, I admit, once the high ended I'm not sure I even remember what we talked about much less could I apply what I learned in the discussion to real living and making a better life, more informed choices, increasing the value and quality of life. That was all done by laying out a line of coke, a shot of agave, bedding down with a babe.

I never really cared about making a better life. Life was what I had at the moment, and I never thought about the future. Whatever was happening was happening. Why change it, I wasn't dead, right? And when you thought about the future, well, you looked out on the world and knew the future ended and started where your hands did, where luck did, where your ability to speak did, where your thoughts did—certainly not in any plan for a better life, no paper or schooling was going to give me a future, a future was something others worked for, others suffered and sacrificed for, what I had would be probably what I would end up with on any given day. There was no intellectual process I applied to improving the quality of my life, and I was not into accumulating goods, no property or money or savings, just the day I woke to and how I would fill the day, what people, what activity, making my way around those in my way, trying to get to the end of it without OD'ing or getting arrested or killed. It was all about having a good time and surviving.

It never even occurred to me to visit a library. Sure, I'd see those homeless lounging around the downtown libraries, I'd see those hundreds of Mexican and Central American mothers with their kids at the libraries, they valued books and education and libraries as the most important resources in life, but back then I didn't have a clue as to the importance of books, libraries, studying, and education.

Man, was I dumb! Mostly due to my arrogance, since up to that point in the early nineties, whatever I touched resulted in success in one form or another—beautiful girlfriend, book contract, movie deal, new house, new cars, even though, now as I look back, it was quite another story: an ugly divorce, piles of unpaid tax bills going unheeded later to come creeping into my life with haunting ferocity and consequences, a dangerous cocaine habit that grew and infiltrated everything I did, new friends that in the end were thieves and predators upending my life.

Perhaps had I even bothered to read a book, which I didn't for years, had I valued books and my career more, which I didn't, had I given any thought at all to my life, I might have seen through my self-imposed deception and changed it, but I didn't.

There were no libraries in my growing up. I never went into one until I had my first kid and I was around thirty. I'd go in like any parent with my first boy, then two years later my second boy and we'd lie around on the floor in the kids' section and leaf through these big hardcover picture books. I'd read to them, laugh, make my voice match the character's action on the page, growl for wolves, chirp for birds, whisper and whistle for wind, grump and groan for dramatic conflicts between the protagonist and villain, usually trying to trap, cook, and swallow an innocent little girl or adventurous boy in the woods.

One day, however, thinking it was time for me to return to my trade as a poet and writer, I thought of doing some research on my cultural history and

I went to the village of Estancia and checked out a book on the history of the plains in that area—el llano estacado, as the Spanish called it. I drove an hour east of Albuquerque and at the town of Moriarty turned south and drove another ten miles across flat prairieland, so flat, in fact, that professional road cyclists from all the world often came to train on it.

I got to the Estancia library, a humble little brick-and-mortar hut. It was the first time I checked out a book. I was excited and looking forward to opening it and reading my history. The only thing I really knew about it was the very limited oral history my grandma shared with me. She said that as a little girl, when they herded the sheep north from Chihuahua to her father's lands, which was called the White Mule Ranch, which is southeastern New Mexico today, she'd often see Mexican Indians lynched from trees and utility poles for miles.

She had Comanche roots, my grandfather's were Tarahumara, and I wanted to know why this happened. I wanted to understand how all this tragedy unfolded and who permitted it, where was the law and where were those people who were supposed to be upholding the law of the land? The Treaty of Guadalupe-Hidalgo between Mexico and the United States guaranteed that on signing the document all lands owned by Mexicans would be respected and honored.

But every single line in the treaty was ignored. The treaty allowed Pinche Gringos roaming in vigilante packs to ransack and raid all they encountered, burning everyone out. I wondered what allowed these outlaw gangs to be written about as heroes, and why was the truth covered up, who wrote these lies, who furthered the deception, how did it get into schoolbooks and novels and heroic poems, what was the purpose of demonizing me and my people? I needed to know and had set my mind on sitting down and doing some serious research to find these answers.

And it was more than a desire to write an epic narrative and see some money, which I was running out of quickly. There was still a place in my heart where I longed to return to my craft, to be the poet I was, to get back on a reading tour, clean up, quit screwing around so much and join the tribe of poets who loved and respected me and wondered about my absence.

But just as the road to hell is paved with good intentions, my road to knowledge was paved with beautiful cobblestones of promises to myself that soon cracked under the heavy traffic of everyday distractions and drop-ins of drug addicts filled with pure bullshit about how they were going straight and never did, how they were going to reunite with families and get a job and never did.

Like me. I was a disgrace to the profession. I never even opened the book. I was not used to reading books, and though my impulse to read was driven by a fierce need to know, the partying life obscured all that. Friends came over, my kids and I always found things to do: go hike at the river, play basketball, go swimming, go to movies, play at the park. And fellow tenants in the apartment complex, with nothing to do, almost never left my apartment.

From time to time I ventured out to do poetry readings. I wrote sometimes. I went out each evening clubbing with Herman, who always had plenty of drugs, which meant that every morning I was hungover and I couldn't have read a stop sign a foot away. In short, I was living a life of supreme dissolution, and as far as being a literary man, well, there was as much literary life and practice in me as was in the derelict passed out by the dumpster.

Then one day I got a notice to appear in court—the library filed charges against me that I had stolen government property. Wow, I was going to court for stealing a library book.

One of my friends, a guy named Squirrel—his father owned a chain of Chicano restaurants and he ran a limo service for titty-bar girls and their after-hours clients—printed a bunch of T-shirts with the message on the back in blazing red, "What's Really Going On" with the outline of a map of Estancia and a star where the library was. We tried to make this issue a political one, we wanted people to think the library was racist, that they were targeting me because they were bigots, against me educating myself. Truth was, it was bullshit—it was my fault, I should have returned the book and been done with it. But when you're doing lots of drugs, shit, you'll do anything to make yourself a hero. Make yourself a revolutionary, an activist for people's rights—I had, in truth, about as much concern for people's welfare or constitutional rights as the glue-sniffer crouched at the bottom of the staircase outside the apartment complex.

Nonetheless, we persisted in our delusion as the people's bad ass vatos out to set shit straight. We all wore the T-shirts and sold a bunch of them on street corners, enough to buy groceries and pay the rent. After an hour of searching I found the book and returned it. Charges were dropped. And after that I was gun-shy of libraries and had no inclination to get within ten miles of one. They were trouble.

And I felt this way, until 9-11 happened and I was sitting in a bar, knocking down a few tequila shots with friends when these people appeared on the TV hanging from the ceiling behind the bartender and I heard this librarian say to her interviewers, "The FBI came in insisting on seeing the books that certain people checked out and I absolutely refused to do so, Patriot Act or no Patriot Act, that was infringement of privacy and I was not going to have it in my library."

Right then and there I had a new heroine. From that moment I considered librarians the bravest warriors in the land, true patriots, defending our right to read books and holding the line on our right to privacy.

And my change of heart toward libraries and librarians was just that, until I got an invitation to visit Salinas, California, where Ms. Elizabeth Martínez was cutting the ribbon on a new library, funded in part by a grant from the Gates Foundation and supported heartily by the mayor, who had to fight off complaints from trust-funders from Monterey Bay and wealthy agricultural growers in the area who feared educating the common populace might get them to thinking and asking for higher wages and better living and working conditions.

I flew out and visited several schools, where I talked about the importance of education and how writing and reading could liberate them from boredom and loneliness.

Then I attended the grand opening.

I really had no idea how I fit into the program, but doubtful as I was about the role of libraries in the community, saying nothing to Ms. Martínez, who believed and worked endless hours to make it the center of the community, I satisfied myself with telling myself I'd give a short talk, get my check, and leave.

But something happened to change my view of libraries. My new commitment was to devote my time to making sure there was a library on every corner on every street in the world. The work on behalf of libraries was my new passion and I'll tell you why.

Elizabeth told me to expect a crowd, I think she said around five or six hundred and I privately doubted her numbers if not outright rejected them as wishful thinking. She also told me they were going to insert one of my poems into a time capsule, along with others' things, to inform people in the future a hundred years from now how we lived and what we did.

There was also a mascot she was proud of and was going to introduce to the audience—a turtle. A small one. A very common turtle. One that you would never stop your car to get if you saw it crawling along a road bank.

I got to the library around one or two in the afternoon and stood around. I went into the brand-new library and looked around. It had a marine theme—fish swam on the walls among painted seaweeds. All kinds of colorful reefs and waves and splashes everywhere. It was very cool. Gave you the feeling that you were on an adventure with Jules Verne and *Twenty Thousand Leagues under the Sea*.

Ms. Martínez was a very smart lady, and a very progressive one. In addition to converting a lazy cynic like me into a passionate advocate for libraries, she was, I learned later, a revolutionary force in the library world.

She had been the national director for the American Library Association. She was the first director to stock multicultural books in every California library. She also had her car bombed in L.A. by a white racist for doing so, and she was threatened by white supremacists in Carmel, but she kept on. And this is a woman who stands no taller than 5'2", very soft-spoken and gentle.

At the end of the library opening day, I was willing to follow her anywhere anytime, to be on call for her for the rest of my life. I stood out there by the door and I watched cars drive in, not new cars but older used cars packed with grandmas and grandchildren and workers and kids and teenagers. They had a football field of booths set up with long tables stretching end to end stacked with free books and I watched these ladies and older women and young kids carry stacks and armfuls of books to their cars and fill the trunks of their cars until they could not fit any more books in them.

And I watched for the next few hours more and more and more people drive in, walk up, crossing fields in groups of ten and twenty and thirty, five and six and seven families grouped together arrive, and the people far outnumbered what Elizabeth guessed might come—she thought around five or six hundred, but as I stood there in awe, there must have been five thousand people and I realized at that moment what I had never even remotely realized before—that yes, the library was the center of the community.

And when that ribbon was cut and I stared at the turtle in the cardboard box, and the mayor spoke, thinking how the turtle would outlive all who were present, wondering what alien might read my poem and wonder about me, Elizabeth cut the ribbon and thousands of families streamed through the library doors, they came in on crutches and wheelchairs, addicts and people who had never done drugs, young and old, all jamming in and went to the computer banks and children's center or ancestry room or the Chicano archives room or classroom where writers were giving workshops or mobbing the desk attendants with questions or grabbing a book and settling into a reading chair, or roaming the aisles of shelved books: at that moment I realized they all felt the library was their home, their place of refuge, where they didn't need money, where they weren't asked for their credit card or ID, where they were accepted and respected and welcomed.

That changed how I thought about libraries forever, and after that day I have spent a good deal of my time on book drives, helping to raise money for libraries, even buying a bookmobile and driving to remote villages in the Southwest to hand out thousands of free books to students and teachers.

Thank you, Elizabeth Martínez.

14.

—

Book Signing

I WAS FEELING GREAT AS I DROVE SOUTH DOWN I-25 to visit Hatch High School. Good for just having my new novel, *A Glass of Water*—set in the southern New Mexico area—published but feeling good also because it could have turned out different. One rule I rarely broke: always show up straight and ready to offer my best side to the people. Once I got up to speak and read I did my best to give them everything I had in my heart, the best of hope and love in me. I never offended anyone by spouting out curse words or demeaning any one. I was always respectful and endearing, generous and charming. Even funny. These Chicano people, Mexicans and fieldworkers, had suffered so much, and they believed in me and I honored them and their hard lives. With the desert not far from where I was speaking strewn with hundreds of corpses of immigrants who journeyed north and died in the attempt and not even a single newspaper then, back in the early 2000s, thinking this national tragedy was important enough to print, I did my best to convey to them that I knew their oppression and neglect and that I was here to write poems about it and hopefully someday when they're published in a book the whole world can know about this nightmare. (And I did it, not only in my book *C-Train*, but also in my book *When I Walk Through That Door, I Am . . .*)

As a confused and lonely teenager I used to want to get in the drug-dealing game, more specifically, smuggling large quantities of weed. It seemed like all the cool kids, the popular ones were slinging weed and they had all the pretty girls. I wanted to be one of them, never dreaming that one day I'd be a poet, and it felt so good right now to be me, four boxes of my novel in the back seat, my beat-up, used Subaru clunking down the interstate. I appraise both sides of the prairie as I pass Belen, where I came out of the orphanage on weekends to visit my cousins. I loved corrals steaming with manure and cows and horses and crows in the elms. I loved the sunlight spreading over the alfalfa fields. I loved life so much back then.

Now I loved it in a different way—after the scars and betrayals, the drug addiction and boozing, the mistakes and failures, my brother murdered and after a terrible divorce in which my ex-wife deceived me every which way possible and took every single thing I had (down to my belts, underwear, socks, everything—she was going to sell them when I got famous), I loved life but in a different way, a quiet from-a-distance way, a way where I didn't intrude or bother anyone.

There were still things to be thankful for, even though I was still relapsing from time to time into my old addiction to cocaine. No one escapes entirely from those days. The curse lingers in the soul forever, like a crack in a windshield where a pebble flew off a gravel truck on the highway and smacked the windshield. It grows and spiders all across the days of your life.

I looked out at the solitary shacks in the distance, converted storage containers with stovepipes and doors added for makeshift homes, clusters of wooden huts and piles of used rubber tires, broken vehicles, almost looked like salvage yards, and I wondered which ones were meth labs camouflaged as beggars' huts.

Didn't take a genius to reason that the cartels owned every gas station between the border and Albuquerque, owned car-part stores, used tire outlets where all the Mexican employees, drenched in gold chains and Rolex watches, changing tires as if that was enough to conceal their covert trade, had new Suburban SUVs; fast-food joints, liquor stores, delivery trucks, and I bet my last nickel that they had dozens of crates of military-grade weapons buried in these sand hills. Bet my second to last nickel the cartel was selling weapons to white supremacists on the military bases that sprawled all around southern New Mexico. No one was surprised when we read about it in the newspaper. Murders, kidnappings, and I would have been caught right in the middle of that shit if a change hadn't come over me.

Now, I was salivating for some of that world-famous Hatch green chile, listening to NPR, imagining myself sitting at one of those four-table small Chicano cafés digging into a huge plate of enchiladas.

First the high school. El Paso and Ciudad Juárez was just a spit and skip away and I thought about all my homies still living there and in the smuggling game, hustling, staying awake at all hours, driving at night, before sunrise, getting that supply and demand shit down to make the car payment and rent and pay child support. Right alongside the most delicate and aromatic cacti blossoms and sweet greens in this arid high desert, the plains hid some evil doings—buried bodies, the detritus of the evil empire that spreads its ugly gangrene where it can.

I drove into Hatch and pulled into the high school parking lot, and it pained me to think about my past. Back then I didn't know what to do with myself, I didn't know I could be useful in any way except to lurk in the dark with other throwaway addicts. There was no such thing as a friend in the drug game. No such thing as honor. No such thing as loyalty. It was about going along with the idiots so you might, at the end of the day, get high. Drugs were everywhere and I intended to talk about that today in my speech, how drugs were the new curse for us Chicanos, the hell that first glimmers with dawn light and ravishes you later with its infernal flames. If you asked me for any amount of drugs, I knew where to get them for you, wholesale quantity, fine, at the best price in America. If you asked me for my résumé, I would look at you like you were speaking Mandarin. What? Résumé? What is that?

Back then I needed time to die slowly, little by little in daily increments; I needed love and in my perverse brain-fucked head I found it in dealing weed. I needed meaning and purpose and found it in baggies of weed. I needed self-esteem and I found it sitting around friends' trailers sharing a bong and drinking beer and wine. Hard to believe I survived those days but I did, and with a strong step and even stronger back, I carried the boxes in and walked into the school gymnasium.

I was met with an amazing crowd, filling the bleachers. Cheerleaders performed for me. A student mariachi band played. Teachers helped as I signed and handed out my book to long lines of students.

I was given all kinds of gifts: baseball caps from a dozen garages and gas stations and mechanic shops, pins advertising the best cafés and the hottest green chile, ballpoint pens and pencils and ribbons and T-shirts each advertising some local business, a *panadería* or menudo breakfast hangout, frozen red and green chile in sandwich bags, stacks of homemade tortillas, and packets of biscochitos.

And after hugging dozens of parents and field-workers and laborers, I took the brimming cardboard boxes I had carried full of books to the car and placed them in the back seat. As I drove out of the parking lot, hundreds of people came out and waved good-bye to me, still thanking me with smiles and tears of gratitude.

An hour or so into my drive north, back to Albuquerque, I flipped the switch on the radio and just then a book reviewer came on NPR. He was talking about my novel, about the fieldworkers and this area and the people I had just come from visiting. He said there were some unforgettable passages in the novel but that the time-structure was confusing and he couldn't recommend it.

I started to curse out loud, speaking aloud to myself in the car how he didn't have a clue about my novel and then I turned the radio off. In the ensuing silence and hum of tires on the road, it then dawned on me that the entire front of my shirt was damp with the tears from the people I was hugging in the gym, and I thought with a wide grin how a bad review was fine, that's okay if you don't like it, the real test of a novel about a place and its people comes from the people and the place.

And they loved it. Enough to drench my shirt with their tears of joy.

A wet shirt and a ho-hum book review are so much better than pharmacy painkiller pills and cocaine and watching out for the police and court appearances and prison terms. I'm going to wear this shirt, I told myself, every time I go out to read, maybe, for the rest of my life, to remind me of what really matters.

15.

Loving Life

My wife threw me out. Said she wanted a divorce and refused to let me sleep in the guest house or even on the couch. She was keeping everything, said, "Take your box of poems and get the fuck out." And I left, borrowed enough money to pay first and last month's rent plus deposit and for the next month or so slept on the carpet, ate fast food with plastic forks and spoons, and wondered what the fuck I was going to do now.

My grandma may not have told me in so many words as much as by her example of living frugally and honestly, that if I was going to write, I should do so from the heart. She never lived long enough to know me as a poet, although she lived to be a hundred.

I had to figure out how to make money, and thank the good Lord just about then a Mexican director contracted me to write a screenplay and add to that invitations from universities came in to do readings that paid well and I was able to buy myself a typewriter and a cheap tape recording machine. I set about making poetry tapes to sell them to bookstores and anyone else in the apartment complex who would buy them.

I went door to door, knocking and talking and selling. I didn't sell any, but I made a lot of friends on heavy medication for bipolar disease and depression, and the very next day half of them took my sales visit as a welcome to come to my apartment and hang out all day. They mostly just sat on the floor and stared at the walls. Some made crosses on the walls with their spit. Others paced back and forth in the kitchen room that also served as living room and everything else except for the bedroom, where I had set up my typewriter and table to work.

My private space. It had a big window looking out on the park across the street and I often stood for a long time looking and brooding about my fucked-up life. It was a great place to stand and feel totally fucked up. Wallow in my misery. Herman would come by as well as others, throw some new supply of drugs on the table, and I would find myself trying it out, your coupon freeloader, I was.

But inside me was this voice that often paralyzed me with guilt and made it almost impossible for me to enjoy my buzz. Write, write from the heart, Grandma implied by her strict example, and so I started. One word, then another, stringing the airy beads together in what would become my best-selling memoir, *A Place to Stand*.

The place had a pool and dry sauna. And the first thing on my mind was to get high with some chick and have sex in the sauna. And I did but it wasn't fun. Near starvation and unable to meet my bills, couldn't pay the rent, couldn't write, parties with people stopping by at night, and then in the morning, when I tried to write, everything was a false start and I kept trashing all my attempts and all I thought about was fucking in the sauna? No wonder my life was a puke bucket overflowing daily. Every day was the same, get high, have sex, make a feeble attempt at writing.

Marlo was one of the tenants, and I wasn't sure why he was so poor and needy but he was. Call him my first faculty or staff resident in the sacred school of nimwits. When my two boys came over for a visit, he convinced me he was an Indian, and we went to Taos and rented a rubber raft and boated down the Taos Box, and the extent of his Indian skills was to lead us the wrong way down the river and then get out and pull us to the shore after we got stuck ten minutes into the ride.

He looked and acted like one of those guys from a TV show about the 1950s—Frankie or Richie; leather jacket, greased hair duck-tailed back, standing in a cool way with polished shoes, had the looks of a Chicano James Dean and a smile like John F. Kennedy.

Then there was Lanzo, the friendly giant who stood seven feet tall and weighed four hundred pounds and was zombied out on serious medication for his schizophrenia. No matter where he stood or sat or lingered, his big forefinger was busy tracing the cross on everything it could touch and reach. When we started our basketball team of loonies, we made him our center—and nobody, nobody fucked with him. He held the basketball in his hand the way a pitcher holds a hardball. They were that big.

Others came by various routes. There was Joker, the rapper kid who stabbed his teacher; Brandy, sixteen, dropout, his gorgeous girlfriend; and me, Marlo, and then the last one, Benny, our in-house Pachuco homie, and we decided to start a tribe. A tribe of six.

And we gathered and printed poems on T-shirts and recorded poetry tapes and Joker and Brandy and Marlo and Benny all went out to hit various downtown street corners and we made our food, gas, bills money, each got his cut from the sales, and the summer didn't seem so bad, even though all of us were rocking on our heels from a recent family sorrow or medical problem, the sunlight and grass smells from the parks and the kids in the pool and the kids on bicycles and women toting armfuls of groceries back the day their food stamps arrived all made life good and we cruised through our problems like a breeze through tall mountain grass.

I invited my friend Robert over and told him to bring his kids. I forgot, in the barrio, when you invite one kid, especially in summer, to come and swim, that the family grows and grows.

The landlord didn't have a problem with my two boys and me and Lanzo in the pool throwing them up in the air so they could dive back into the water. Lanzo would loft them high as a diving board did and they'd come back hitting the water squalling with joy.

But then I'm standing on the balcony one morning and reminiscing back to the days of the orphanage when in summer the young kids were the first ones to hit the pool for swimming lessons. The water at that time of the morning was frigid. Made our lips and fingers turn purple. All of us kids sniffed long boogers hanging from nostrils, over our lips, and we wiped them away across our little brown faces. Made our teeth chatter and bones shiver and our limbs tremble with arctic cold.

But it didn't matter. Skinny as we were, and underfed and abandoned by parents and society, the swimming pool made us feel like normal kids, in our ragged swimming trunks too tight or falling off, skinny legs and ribs showing, shoulder bones jutting out like back ends of starved cows, and as kids do sometimes, one pooped in the pool and as the turd floated up kids yelled and screamed and we all ganged out in a massive fire-drill dash out of the water; and other times when the nuns weren't watching a group of us young hoodlums climbed over the fence and ran for our lives across the watermelon patches, by the KQEO radio towers that played oldies that would have me for hours holding my transistor radio to my ears listening to the Ramones and Richie Valens, and as good as sitting on the irrigation ditches and dreaming of our parents, of a home, of losing ourselves, we sat at the sandbox where we stacked marble pyramids and drew a line ten feet away and like carnies, hooted come and try your luck come and try your luck, and kids lined up and knelt in the dirt and tried to hit the piles and those who did got the four marbles, and good as sailing up high like a comic book hero, flying above the others as they snapped their swing chains and ours was laid over theirs and when they snapped, the kid with the chain overlapping theirs was sent flying and sometimes we lost our grip and sailed and landed breaking arms and shoulder bones. Oh yes, the cold glimmering water shook us to the core with icy teeth-clacking bone chill, but we were never so happy, earth-bound and planted in our joy like a weed under the summer sun at noon, just being so true as kids.

And standing there on the balcony and recalling this, my elbow leaning on the railing, looking lazily at the park mothers with their infants on a blanket crawling over legs, to my right I see Robert turn the corner and behind him a line of forty or so kids trailing with towels, all wearing trunks, all coming to swim and that was when the landlord said enough was enough—all the tenants enjoying a nice cool dip in the pool had to leave as the kids bombarded the pool, cannonballing in, diving in, kicking midair and splashing in, wrestling with and slapping each other and laughing and yelling and whooping and loving life and trying to drown each other.

I don't remember us caring about clothes, sickness, food, or all the shit that had happened to some like getting raped or beaten or being left on some street corner or motel lobby waiting for an addicted mother who said she'd come right back and never again appeared. Despite all this, we were the happiest kids could be clutching our hands together and cringing naked from the cold, without towels, like naked infants just born on a summer morning on an ice floe.

16.

Divide and Conquer Mentality

I'M THE FIRST TO ADMIT THAT I HAVE FALLEN FROM GRACE several times, but never once in my life have I ever hurt a child. I've never even spanked my kids, not once. It comes from being beaten as a child and from knowing so many kids who were molested and beaten. So you can imagine how outraged and shocked I was when a group of Catholic and Jehovah's Witness ladies down in El Paso labeled my poetry as porn and accused me of pedophilia (these monkeys will take a shot at you hanging from their limbs, so be careful where you walk, they're liable to piss on your head—no qualms about relieving themselves of their childhood neurosis in public).

The first incident happened in El Paso. I was giving a talk on education to a group of around a hundred teachers and everything was going well until I quoted an excerpt from a Bukowski poem about how he loves big-ass Mexican women. I thought it was a great poem and that the audience would be delighted, but no, the church had corrupted their love for their bodies.

I thought it would make the women in the crowd clap and bump fists and slap high fives. I loved it. Most of the women in the audience were big-bootie mamas, and like Bukowski, I thought their amplitude was a gift, not a slight. But apparently some didn't.

I think it was the fervid religious conservatives who objected, though not one of them raised their hand to demand an apology (which I would have given outright since I thought it was a compliment, but if not, okay); but no one rose to inform me it was an insult to them. Only later, when I walked over to the superintendent's office to meet him, did I learn that a complaint was lodged with his office that I was rude and evil.

Apparently, a group of die-hard big-mama Catholic women, I assume really frustrated with their sex lives (as who wouldn't be considering the chastity-gag belts they have to wear), charged me with being obscene. My excesses have touched almost every realm but never child abuse.

But it wasn't the superintendent who mentioned it to me. He smiled and shook my hand and gave me a seat in a leather chair and we had coffee and talked a little about education. Instead, it was my host who told me later, after we left the office, that it was a terrible thing I did quoting Bukowski, that I should never do that, ending that I had fallen to new lows. I wasn't angry as much as I was disappointed. In them. How could they not love Bukowski's poem?

Wow, was all a voice in my head was saying, never seen such reactions from a group, teachers or not, but somehow I was feeling that my host was really at the center of this censorship—though he was a really cool dude, took care of his ailing mother, played piano in the evenings at a coat-and-tie bar, he was divorced and religiously extreme in his views on sinners and saints. I fell into the sinner category. I didn't feel ashamed; consternation and regret was what I was feeling, consternation over the fact that we Latinos hate our bodies and are ashamed of them and regret that these teachers are going into classrooms every day and sharing their shame of their bodies with kids, destroying for the kids the chance they have of loving their bodies.

Later that day, when I was talking to a hundred teachers in the cafeteria, I could see out the window into the parking lot and I saw, with some alarm, FBI agents parking their unmarked government cars and striding into the school. Holy shit, I thought, I'm being arrested?

I learned later they arrested the super for embezzlement, handcuffed him, read him his Miranda rights, and escorted him out of the office. My host claimed he knew nothing about what was going on, though they were best friends.

Just goes to show there's room for all kinds of people in this world, those who disapprove of salacious excerpts from a poet's work, and those who would prefer to keep their secrets private and unwritten, hidden from the light of the world.

Called hypocrisy. Called religious oppression. Called teaching us to hate our bodies. I still love his poem and still love big-booty mamas.

But you won't believe the extreme distance their religious hysteria goes, it spreads like a PBS Nazi documentary that depicts blood spilling over a map of Eastern Europe—yup, soon as they read a poem of mine in my new book, they spread a poem of mine through the internet and the rumor starts that I was a pedophile and here's why.

Not long before my El Paso keynote, a book of poetry of mine was published, *The Esai Poems*, and a poem therein has to do with my son taking a bath when he was a toddler, playing and splashing in the tub with a yellow rubber ducky and soap bubbles.

I was doing all kinds of little domestic jobs around the house and popping in and out of the bathroom to check on my boy. When I got done I undressed and took a shower in our other bathroom and wrapped a towel around my waist and when I heard him calling me, I ran wet and naked, sopping foot puddles on the wood floor in my trail, to the far end of the house to my bedroom where the tub was.

As I entered the bathroom, I cooed are you done little birdie, are we all done and he splashed and giggled and kicked that he wanted to bathe more and stay a little longer in the tub.

As I bent to grab and pull him out of the water my towel fell off and when I turned and leaned over to get the towel and wrap it around me, he laughed and stared at my butt and then my penis.

He touched himself and pulled his penis. Splashed. Slapped the water. I did a little dance, naked, and turned and danced and he laughed so hard he started hiccupping. I shook my hips and swerved and slid back and back and forth, while uttering nonsense dah-doo-doo-doos, scubee-lookieees-moonies, and he cracked up so hard the poor little thing fell back into the water and must have swallowed water and been disoriented for a few seconds because when I pulled him and sat him upright in the water, he had that look of exasperation and what the hell just happened.

Then he came back to his senses, grinned at me and searched between my thighs with his eyes for the perky little worm that gave him such pleasure to look at.

It was cheaper and more fun entertainment seeing his aging father dancing around in the bathroom slipping and heel-toeing on the black and white tiles than hiring a bus full of clowns.

Well, leaving all this aside for the moment, the book sold well and then one day I get an email from Las Cruces and it's from an NMSU professor claiming I'm a pedophile, that I should be arrested and charged and put in stocks and in jail. They're the same fist-banging ladies that fiercely raged against Bukowski's poem excerpt (and then later his book—listing it, and later banning it, as they did mine, from the schools).

I'm not altogether sure why I didn't respond to their name-calling at first, and now as I remember it, I suppose I was busy or maybe it was that such nonsense begs for an audience and not to give it one hurts more than to recognize the issues as sensible and with any iota of purpose or worth—not sure.

But I didn't. I was simply shocked that they took this beautiful experience I had with my son and darkened it with their infected, sinister minds. It shows me how much damage the church has done to us when we think of our bodies, and more importantly, when we try to teach our kids that our bodies are beautiful and honored lovely blossoms we must enjoy and compliment. Never a reason for condemnation or shame, as they would have it.

One thing, however, I am so very happy about: my son, now a teenager, loves his book and laughs just as hearty now reading that penis poem as he did as a toddler. And he loves his body.

17.

Our Bodies

A GREAT PART OF MY LOVE AND APPRECIATION for our bodies stems from my early-morning meditations and reading Tibetan scripture. I broke the cycle of abuse. We were taught to hate our bodies by those religious fanatics that came west with homesteaders, pilgrims, and frontiersmen. In their colonial genocide, to somehow alleviate their guilt and help themselves justify their pillaging, they taught us children that we were a subhuman species. They despised life.

But no one escapes the sins of their fathers. No one. White nationalists and supremacists were the unfortunate heirs of their criminal ancestors, and now, because the white man is unwilling to deal with the historical injustice, their children are dying from opiates, going to prison daily for grabbing rifles and killing schoolchildren, losing their jobs, and still, still will not deal with their racism—it's a case of the sins visiting their sons and daughters.

But shortly after this, a month or two after, just coming out of a rough winter, I was invited to a charter school on Albuquerque's West Side, a unique charter school for kids who couldn't deal with mainstream high school. These were kids the system had classified as bad boys and girls, making their own choices in the limited life they had, crossing borders and barriers as easily as they told authority figures to fuck off.

I liked and respected them.

A week previous to this, just as snow had faded from the ground in Santa Fe, I had given a talk at a monastery there. Normally, I steer away from any of these spiritual casinos—you gamble your salvation, and your chances of entering heaven are equal to the amount of money you toss on the table or basket.

Anyway, so there I am lecturing in front of a hundred or so robed Buddha followers sitting on butt cushions with Hindu murals on the walls and candles burning and the meeting room all nicely constructed with fresh vigas and wicker curtains and stone tiles . . . well, in a word, beautiful.

It inspired me to believe briefly in fellowship, notwithstanding that everyone in the audience was white and I had a sense they didn't have to worry about utility bills. They had inherited money, didn't work, or if they did, did so to stave off boredom.

I dismissed my impulse to lecture them on correcting historical justice—for penance they could redeem their forefathers' tyrannical slaughter of people of color (Mexican Indio in this case) by just dropping their long overdue payment into my hat.

My kids and wife were pleased, as they normally saw me talk in front of standing-room-only university auditoriums or prisons and here I was with a blessed congregation of monks, and I spoke about my time imprisoned in an isolation cell for years and how I left my body and traveled through the universe, and how I felt God, then touched God, then traveled with God. God spoke to me many times. I meant every word of it too.

Before I left I met this woman who wanted to work with me, or at least attend one of my classes to learn from me. I agreed and a week later she was sitting in class in civilian clothes.

Earlier that morning she flew into Albuquerque from Denver. It was a bright clear blue sky day and the school had a vibrant atmosphere to it. I walked in and led her with me, and we both entered a classroom and took our seats and when the students came in I started with them.

Her demeanor set her apart from us, it was refined and cautious, punctuated with a heavy layer of decorum and caution. And became even more so, as the kids filed in, cursing, somber, untrusting, and even mocking with their dismissive glares at us, serious-faced kids aged between twelve and fifteen who had already done some serious shit. A few of them had just been released from Juvey Hall that morning.

To break the ice, I told my class two stories, but first I gave the lay of the land. Some of you are going to write a poem, others, those of you who can't write that good and feel better illustrating and drawing, are going to compliment the poems with your sketches.

But first, the stories: I was working with a kid once who thought he was rotten through and through. I told him no one is completely rotten, there's good in all of us. Especially kids, so don't be so harsh and quick to judge yourself. Just because a lot of fucked-up adults label you as no good, seems to me, they're talking more about themselves than you.

Anyway, this kid was going to shoot himself. I walk down into the basement of his house one morning and catch him standing there with a pistol in his lap. I tell him I'm not going to stop him from blowing his brains out, but I ask him to stand in front of the mirror. I tell him to hold the pistol to his temple and kill the part of himself that's no good but not harm the good part. Can you do that, brother?

Of course he couldn't. I told him all we gotta do is work on getting more of the good part of ourselves to come out and more of the bad shit to leave, and he got it. He couldn't shoot without hitting the good stuff in him— memories, feelings, whatever.

Another time, I'm finished with visiting a secure-setting lockup for federal prison kids down in southern Arizona, and I go back to my hotel and find a bunch of RVs and big trucks with flags flapping from antennas and decals on doors advertising they're Patriotic Tea Partiers. I'm like what the fuck?!

Then after picking up the paper in the lobby I read they're here to keep Mexicans out, to fight for liberty and justice and such ho-hum shit. Too much TV, I thought, The Rifleman and John Wayne clogged up their arteries and they needed an enema. I was just the person to give it to them.

Through the fall and spring I'd been reading Thich Nhat Hanh and Chogyam Trungpa and trying to follow their approach and example and so the following morning when the dining area was packed with all these puffy-cheeked white middle-aged cowboy-hat-wearing men with red bandannas around their sunburned necks, I started my peaceful kindness protest based on serving others.

I went table to table asking if they needed more coffee, how about pancakes, juice, cereal, and almost everyone needed fill-ups or refills on their plates and I was busy there for a while but as it died down I had a little time to myself and I stacked my plate with fruit, yogurt, English muffins, and then I sat at a table with these proud Americans.

It didn't go well. They asked me to move, warned they'd report me to management for dereliction of duty and bothering patrons and such. But I said, I rent a room too, I'm not an employee, like you, I'm a guest. I just wanted to be friends.

And they packed their plates and cups and left the table, and I went to the next table and the next table, trying to be sociable and civilized, a citizen, spreading the good neighborly word of love and respect. But they wouldn't have it.

And I emptied out the restaurant. And I thought, thinking of Thich Nhat Hanh, Trungpa, this kindness works—all the fighting and fisticuffs wouldn't have cleared them out, and me serving them did the job.

I decided after breakfast that I would buy cases of bottled water and hit the trenches and meet them at the border, hand out water and sit on their tailgates and talk turkey. Just maybe I could clear them off the border.

The kids in the class loved the story. And after my comic rendition of how to handle conflict in a peaceful manner, I gave them an assignment to write a poem of defiance or apology and every single kid wrote on defiance.

But my guest, I'll call her Miss Rosa, didn't, and when she read her poem, it disturbed the class quite a bit. She introduced herself as a Buddhist student and told them that she had been studying Buddhism for years.

Most of the kids in class had written poems or sketched a picture with an edge—gangster rap, violence, weapons, early deaths of friends, grief, teardrops, drugs, boyfriends, the chaos of being lost in a parentless world, prison or juvenile camps, cultural symbols of pride, and so on. So when Miss Rosa read about how sorry she was, sorry to everyone for what she had done, the kids figured (correctly in some cases) that they had done much worse but didn't need to apologize to anyone.

Fuck them, was the general refrain, and since they had taken a liking to shy and self-effacing Miss Rosa, they were, as they called it, backing her play. Giving her *esquina*, got her back. Their loyalty expressed itself by their fuck you's to the people she wanted to apologize to.

Then she explained herself and the poem. For eight years she was a policewoman in San Diego, and every night on her shift they went out routinely and found Mexicans and Chicanos and beat them to bloody pulps in alleys. That's what I'm sorry for, for hurting those kids, for beating them with my club every night for years.

The air in the room suddenly chilled. Their faces turned down and grimaced with explosive rage. They were caught in a maelstrom of confusion: a minute ago they liked and respected her, now they realized she had been a cop and worse, used her authority to hurt them. She was the enemy.

A couple of kids she had stood over earlier and helped to draw and give them advice, since she was an artist, and helped them in their designs, murmured under their breath fuck you and tore up the sketches.

Then everyone sat still as the room filled with a heavy water of silence, as if someone was filling it with water that would soon drown us all.

Then one of the tougher kids, one that had gotten out of Youth Authority that very morning, and was an unspoken leader in the group, said it was okay, it was in the past. He reluctantly smiled at her, still hurt by what he took as a betrayal, but he forgave her. We move on he said, we change.

She was crying.

Another girl she helped said shit to the past, fuck it, just don't be doing that no more.

Another one said it's all good, but man, man, how could you do it, how could she do that?

And so it went when the bell rang, and everyone got their poems and drawings and left.

I stayed behind and left only after I knew everyone was okay and when I got to the outside door that opened to the parking lot, there was a scuffle with a teacher or security guards or something and I noticed it was one of the girls in my class. And when I approached, the girl turned to me and said fuck this shit, I drew this in his class, you liked it, fuck you, you can't and ain't taking my drawing.

The teacher claimed it was gang graffiti, not allowed, they had to confiscate it and they did and the girl fought back to get it and they handcuffed and arrested her and dragged her in the back of a patrol car and she stared at me with hurt, confused eyes through the back window as they drove away and I knew those sad eyes would never trust again. Something in me at that moment reaffirmed my struggle to reform what we thought of as education. No more ignoring what I just saw. No more ignoring these kids. What was missing in my life at that moment was that girl's face in the back of the patrol car looking at me through the reinforced wire glass—her eyes questioning my integrity, as if saying, well, as least I have the guts to fight for what I think is right. And you?

Later that day, searching for an answer to this crazy hubris I'd been experiencing recently in educational settings, I got to thinking about the body. My body. I thought about the morning my son discovered his penis and laughed with such delight that I could only imagine an angel laughing so hard in the abundant light of Jesus's embrace. I still hear that green-tree-whiplashed-in-breeze laughter, that soft leaning of field grass in a gentle caressing of prairie wind laughter, that of a young four- or five-year-old boy lavishing song-love on himself for the miraculous revelation of his body, his hands, fingers, penis, little chest, small knobby knees, eyes burning so bright with life-light that they lit the room up and made it brighter in their own dawn sunrise of awareness.

That laughter over time dwindles to whisper and then silence as society, especially religion and these muck-eating religious demons, spread their venom, howling how the body is bad, how lust is wrong, how we should be ashamed and atone for our sins for having a cock and pussy.

If the words *fuck 'em* ever had a context to squeeze out every drop of their meaning, it's now, when applied to those hypocritical broken-spirited and evil-minded religious revelers in their sanctimonious shit.

The body is so beautiful. So amazing to think that it works so well, given the trillions of cells, the various organs, the ability to move and stream and turn and lift and lay and jump and do all the things that its needs to do to live in a day. It transcends any reasoning, its rises to the level of a miracle, an unutterable and divine gift from the legions of saints and lords that inhabit the air we breathe.

And yet, some of the bestial-brain scum have the ignorance to denounce it. To cage it. To punish it. To devour it when young in their loathsome and abominable self-hatred that they spew on the innocent.

A week or so later I'm getting ready to go give a talk at the Detention Center for Youth Offenders. I finished up wiring the electrical cords and running them under the carpeting of our bedroom and into a closet that would be my new office to write in. I taped the wire ends, covered them with plastic nuts, showered, dressed and took off.

Standing before a crowd of a hundred or so young gangbangers, I started talking about how I was learning to love myself, respect my body.

"What I'm going to talk about today may upset some of you but I think it's a valid topic, one that's hardly ever discussed—and that is the sensual side of us criminals, the sexual part of us is never touched upon. They have oodles of shows with women in orange jump suits and women dykes with three-foot dildos and women kissing and loving each other but there's never been one that explores the erotic side of convicts.

"You can tune into the Escape channel and any other prime-time channel and be assaulted by criminals and convicts killing, murdering, savaging innocent children and citizens. It's as if convicts were exempt from being endowed with any sexual urges or sensual affection. No intimacy. If they do show any emotional side or display affection, it's suspect and exploited for dramatic purposes by the media into a viral rapist cultured in a hog-manure lagoon.

"Look, I wasn't always that in touch and affectionate with myself, there was a time when I was locked up when I hated my body, hated it verbally, physically, spiritually, and mentally. If I'd been nurtured in a healthy environment, hell, I would never have need of health insurance, wouldn't need to grovel before health insurance companies and beg for coverage I can't afford.

"When I was a kid, I discovered the pleasures of stroking my dick, and nuns had to send a SWAT team in after me to break the toilet stall door down to the boy's dormitory bathroom and use battering rams to get into my toilet stall where I was gasping in masturbation.

"And for punishment I was taught my evil appendage was a curse, that it condemned me, that it exiled me to the nether reaches of hell forever and I'm reluctant to admit to myself the detrimental effect it has had on me and how much shit it has caused in trying to compensate for being a sex-crazed deformity.

"For penance, I ate only fish sticks and potatoes for a month. I also had to pray a hundred Hail Marys and Our Fathers on my rosary before each of the stations of the cross, which presented me with an even more dire dilemma: how could I possibly look up and not notice his loincloth and not think about what lay under it? At every station, no matter how many times I thumped my chest with mea culpas and knelt until my kneecaps burned, that idea grew and consumed me until I felt like fleeing from the chapel, an evil plague-carrying sinner.

"From the stations I had to move on to dust the side altars, and this was worse, for the statues were of Mother Mary and Our Lady of Guadalupe—I kid you not, a day cleaning those saints and I knew I was the filthiest maggot-infested monster alive. I deserved death, but not until I was stripped of my skin inch by inch and then flogged until the meat was stripped down to the bones and then my bones were hammered to splinters into a heap of tiny thorns and dumped into a cesspool.

"As an adolescent, I avoided all talk about sex, fearing God was omniscient and would strike me dead. All my friends were drawing big-dicked cartoons during catechism, while the novitiates were screwing some of the kids, while older kids were fucking younger kids under dorm bunks, while others were raping and being raped, while the priest was having kids suck his dick in the sacristy, I closed my eyes and ignored it all. It didn't exist. I prayed. I wanted to be a child filled with piety and chastity, a devoted follower of the heavenly truth.

"It was undiluted trauma that seized my six-year-old heart and stung every nerve until sections of it were dead or paralyzed in a comatose state and I vowed never to infect my child and repeat the disaster. I suggest we quit punishing and measuring for acceptance and demeaning our bodies and teach our kids to love their little bodies that brought them into this world.

"Let us praise our first exploration into the world—seeing sunlight for the first time, inhaling the chill dawn and feeling the night air, tasting our fingers, our beautiful brown eyes mesmerized by their first sight of a field flower, a bird, a tree, reaching out to touch cold creek water for the first time, our first attempts at standing on two feet, our first smile when a dog licks our cheek, let us celebrate the small miracles of our bodies as they move and feel and taste and listen to the world around us with awe—discovering the unutterable mystery of being human. We can do that now as teenagers, because we were never given the right to do so as kids.

"But instead, what do we have?

"One aspect of life that passed before my eyes and ears was the emergence of violent men of the night, who during the day seemed normal, but when nightfall came, they transformed into hideous beasts in excruciating pain and madness; the averted eyes, the steamy effervescence of aggression from an unseen wound that perspired its toxic venom from their pores and enveloped them with dark secrets; they couldn't be described as human, they were something else—half human/half alien—they were dark rooms where vestiges and traces of their humanity were emitted in gnashing teeth, sobs, painful groans, and I could sense they hurled themselves against the walls seeking escape from the solitude, willing to give and do anything to join humanity and be sane, social, accepted and loved, but the meaning of their manhood was damaged, corrupt, and mangled the softer side of them never admitted.

"They made me think deeply about my life because they were my family—my uncles and aunts and brother and sister and parents. There's a radical love that infuses them, the kind I see in the golden leaves of cottonwoods, leaves once green, fully complacent in their green life, to be jolted by a deeper archetypal calling to their true nature as its gets colder and a reverberation of burning love swells in the center of all life and ebbs and flows out urging us into new ways of being."

I can't tell you I know their hearts—the addicts and convicts and homeless—because it would mean I give you the meaning of life and I don't know that. I do know their sexual identity, forbidden and oppressed, holds the key to their self-destruction, that how they feel and think of their most intimate aspect of their bodies was cauterized by molten cattle brands and smudged out—the relationships with their mothers, girlfriends, siblings, children, littered with chaos and violence.

"I want you all to pull some paper out and write a letter to your wives or girlfriends, tell them how much you love them, how much you care and what you're going to do with her when you get out."

After a while, I asked them to read their letters and they sounded so much like mine to Lila.

I resumed, "After hearing you read some of your letters, I see you use words like *bitch*, *gonna fuck you*, *gonna make you my ho*, and you describe taking them down on your car hoods, wherever you want to get off however you want—but you know what?

"It's rape. You're raping the woman you love."

"You better shut the fuck up," one said.

"You're crossing the line, asshole," another said.

"Be best you shut the fuck up," another warned.

I picked up again, "Some of you are going to go to prison, and when you walk through those gates there'll be men who are going to do to you what you did to your girlfriends, you wanna call that love?"

A big Chicano boy got up and went to the bathroom stall and punched the divider-wall so hard he ripped it off its hinges. I ran in and found him about ready to rip the toilet out.

"I didn't mean to rape her, man. I love her . . . I love my *vieja*, but that's what I was taught, man . . . that's what I was taught."

"I know, I know, it's not your fault, I was the same way, even worse, I thought love was beating and whipping and dominating a woman. I was fucked up, vato. Fucked up."

I took my homie back to the class with me and apologized. "I'm sorry. I didn't mean any disrespect to you guys, just wanted to point out that what we learned was how to rape our sisters. And it's not our fault but we can learn how to love, how to be gentle with ourselves and those we love.

"Now I want you all to write another letter apologizing to the babe you love, tell her you didn't mean to hurt or disrespect her, it's what you were taught love was."

I wanted to tell them more but I had already rattled them too much. I wanted to tell them there's so much purposely imposed suffering in the world, so many embittered breaks in every person's life, that their dark lives, their criminal lives, their homeless and impoverished lives staunch the bleeding but never close the wound.

Whispered lives, that if we listen, are a revelation for us that courses above ground like those acequias, like those calls of children at the school-bus stop, like the leaves, the burials of gangbangers, the bleak pistol shots in the deep of night, it seems their lives break down the separations and call the convicts, the poor, the addicts, the hopeless and the mean-spirited to gather and praise life, praise the worthiness of pain and sorrow, make of it something to bind them all into a grateful crowd of brothers and sisters, unrelenting in their belief that God's love can see them through the darkest hours.

I wanted to tell them, "Your lives allow us to rest our heads for a moment and sigh with relief that we are loved when we have always believed we are not lovable; your life sets the intellect aside and allows the heart to speak and what it says is: your heart has room for the thousands of Mexican orphans whose parents were killed by cartels, bring the lonely and forsaken and wandering souls lost in their misery of addiction and targeted by racists as inhuman, bring those who exist in silence and you will speak for them, you will cry out for them with righteous indignation; your lives are a field-worker's song of love and for every hand that reaches for the plant stalk, every hand that works the furrow, every hand that wipes the sweat from the face, every hand that pinches thorns from flesh, every hand that grips cell bars waiting for freedom, every hand that does injury to themselves, every hand that clasps another's hand in *carnalismo*, is what the body represents, is what allows each of you to lift yourself up off your knees and keep walking. Your flesh, your sexual intimacy, your lack of being treated with kindness as children is what this [I sweep the front of my body with my hands] lives with, constantly trying to understand itself. To me, you are my heroes!"

18.
—

A Look Back

THE INCLINATIONS OF THE HEART ARE THE WORST, aren't they, when they wrap around you like a python and constrict you from living, even from moving sometimes, paralyze you the way unrequited love does a lover who doesn't get back the love she's putting out. You could say it's youthful angst, something we're supposed to get through when we're young, but try telling that to someone in the claws of love that's not being returned. Try.

Why I open with this is because of a woman who always wanted to be with me and never could be. I guess this essay is about what never was, the never-could-be's.

To this day, February 24, 2019, she still loves me. She left the United States to live in Mexico, she even married. But none of it slowed her down. She continued staying up till all hours of the night and emailing all her girlfriends to spread rumors and spiteful gossip, with every vowel hell-bent on destroying me.

It didn't work, of course. An undying love does more harm to the purveyor of harmful gossip than to the intended receiver. The assailant becomes the victim, the conspiracy turns on the conspirator, the blade turns back on one.

One obsessed is one who cannot think clearly. So the decades have piled up on each other and she still pines away in some quaint Mexican village, obsessing over writing sonnets and looking out the window at the sea.

I sometimes read of her receiving another award (she has a steamer chest full), see her standing in photo ops in the pages of literary mags, smiling, holding up another check for years of cooing flatteries and complimentary postcards caroling the beauties of philanthropies, and all the good dinners and banquets have made her swell up, a bit long and pudgy in the nose, eyes set deeper into her fleshy folds, beadier, and I wonder, away from the adulation and cameras, how she is doing in her silent hours when all the fan fluff and cameras and interviewers have gone.

I wish her the best. Even more so after skimming through her last book. The book is crafted in such a way as to not offend the reviewers, in keeping with her oh-so-sweet demeanor, appealing to her financial patrons; but it happens, you know, anytime a writer starts writing to please and not explore or experience something new in the work, something harsh and even violent, when that's no longer an aspect of the work, well, suddenly it is cold and drab as leftover oatmeal on the stove.

I met her around the time I wrote *Working in the Dark*, where I detailed my journey into literacy, starting by stealing my first book from the hospital director's office where I worked as a night maintenance man. The book was 450 years of Chicano history in pictures.

It tells you what you need to know about my early years as a budding poet, how the pictures affirmed my existence, how they rendered hope unto me, in some mystical fashion, igniting the embers in my sapling soul.

I was a street kid and free as a bird and I could have gone anywhere, moved to Mexico, where living was cheaper, but I couldn't turn my back and flee from the battles in the streets. And while she did, she didn't leave her memory of me nor her dream of being with me behind. I spurned her advance in the same way I continue to do now with an offer to lunch with an oil executive, bankers and wealthy real estate officers and politicians who vote to outfit our civic patrolmen with military-grade weaponry against citizens who march for their rights.

I stayed in the gristle-mill, continue to defend the battered and abused and embittered poets and teachers and writers who daily suffer indignities in our schools, barrios, the reservations, trying to salvage a little of what they can of our children's future, wielding their literacy, their books, their dreams, under the duress of poverty, administrative opposition, they trudge ahead, teaching our kids to read and write so one day they can voice their opinions on political affairs, so they will vote in ways that improve their chances for survival, even as clouds of toxic pollution from oil companies loom on the horizon and darken our skies and lungs and minds with shareholders' profits. With inexhaustible perseverance, penniless, they don their coats each morning and move into the war zones and reach out to those kids to help them achieve their potential.

I gave up love to go in the direction of people who were fighting for their dignity. For their right to exist.

19.

On Becoming a Poet

PEOPLE WILL DO WHAT THEY DO, grab as much of the bounty as they can for themselves, and when they leave office, vanish as quickly as they appeared. I'm not making a moral judgment; I am simply pointing out that this culture of greed has imposed a severe hit on good people trying to create a healthy society and practice upstanding citizenship while our political rats scurry pocket to pocket nibbling holes in people's pockets, pilfering as much money as they can.

Like the man in his mid-sixties obsessed with exercise, thinking if he does enough of it, he'll reverse the aging trend. He'll slow it, for sure, improve his chances for enjoying his twilight years with better health, but get younger, no. And so you see him, at the health food store, at the gym, buying equipment and weights and expensive exercise and workout clothes all in the belief that he's getting younger with each day. And like him, I suppose shareholders and the wealthy able to afford investments believe that with more money comes immortality.

Reading books and writing imparts aspects of immortality but if you learn alone as I did, though it teaches you to reach into other people's lives and speak with them in your heart, in the privacy of your own mind, reap their insights, even adopt their words as your muse to guide you through this tangled society, it won't help you speak to other people better. Or make friends or be more sociable. In fact, most of my relationships, with women especially, were based on silence and assumptions and hardly any discourse or exchange of words—enough, however, to create intimacy.

Years ago, in *Working in the Dark*, I wrote an essay titled "Past Present," detailing how I learned to read under a blanket with a flashlight in the county jail and then prison. It wasn't, as some might suspect, radical books that first opened my heart and taught it to fly and dream and hope—it was an anthology of romantic poets, it was the Russian novelist Turgenev, it was Emerson, Thoreau, the Black Mountain poets, the California writers, the Mexican and Latin American poets.

Despite all the reading I did, I was still an outsider. That cloud that covered the sky and cast darkness over the land was still with me. I was working like a welder in an underground cavern among vats of molten steel, my welder's mask on, the flame in my hand cutting through thick iron, sparks and bits of iron aflame flying everywhere.

The dark cloud cast its pall over all I did, and yes, I had a marvelous gift for loving words, for crawling up inside the shell of words and seeing life from inside the word, seeing people from within my protective shell of language, but it didn't mean I knew anything, didn't mean I knew how to live or interact with people, and the whole world thought I did.

After all, who can compose such beautiful poems and not know the world? It makes no sense. Certainly, if you can read Lorca, Sabines, Hernández, you know the world, you are aware of how to sit and converse with people. But I didn't. I was at the bottom of this great darkness, buried in sand where things that have been destroyed and shattered and cannonballed go to die, and that's where I lived, where I came from.

I learned from that great darkness that haunted me for decades, reaching its gloved hand over my eyes, I wandered, fooling people I met, pretending I knew how to move about society. And after a lot of self-destructive days and nights I thought would never end, after being caught in this terrible cage of darkness, made of dark bars, dark floor, I existed sightless, scratching at the dark, and little by little, grinding my teeth, breathing as if I might choke, pacing, I began to believe there might be light on the other side of darkness and I prayed and meditated and one day the light, a very faint, momentary breath of light expelled itself and I knew I was absolutely conscious of another way of living where I could climb out of this dark hole and walk, as a human, on the surface of the earth like the others.

By then I lived second to second, buzzed for years. And when I did coke, the veil of darkness draped my soul, I felt a heavy unfolding of material from the dark other world wrap around me, I went deep in this tunnel of darkness and I feared even whispering or breathing. I stayed quiet like a forest animal lodged in its burrow with the wolf breathing just outside, so close I could hear it inhale.

What I meant by working in the dark was that I lived day to day without mooring to the outside world's rules and morals. I had no reference point to guide my behavior or plan my future by, I was tossed and flung out on the great sea of darkness with no light, no stars no moon to light my way or navigate to civilization.

I wrote *Working in the Dark* in three weeks in a hotel room while we were filming *Blood In/Blood Out* in San Quentin. It was a sad and lonely time. Women gave me rides and wanted to have sex halfway to my destination. Agents flocked to me, leaving me wondering how they knew where I had my morning coffee and how they knew who I was as they stepped directly to my table and made offers. Agents, with the exception of a few, with their massively inflated egos, waited for me at my hotel lobby and immediately offered all kinds of enticements to sign with them, some legal, others not.

It was a huge affair, this business of being a poet and screenwriter and gifted orator, and had I known how to waltz with the devil and sleep with angels, maybe it would have worked.

But the cloud, after each night of revelry or debauchery or power-grandstanding, the cloud hovered above my shoulders and head and darkened my path with its ever prophetic and sinister tale of how I must live and work in the dark.

I simply didn't know how to find the doors out of the torture, out of the thousand-mirror room, out of the embrace of death's passionate wooing.

I couldn't save myself and had never rescued myself as others did, in a safe and proper way, the socially acceptable way. I loved teasing death, was fascinated with tempting the demon that lurked in the dark cloud. There was no school to flee to and sign up for classes. No mom and pop to go home to. No grounding point. Just the universe of society that was expanding and exploding with every step I took in it, women, writing commissions, family dilemmas, renovating my house, bad marriage, lack of money or too much money, a galaxy expanding and creating as many new stars and black holes, and me, stumbling through the universe with a rocket, without earth, without humans, without reason or direction, an endless floating and disconnection haunting me every morning I woke up, never knowing what lay ahead, in denial about the pain and hurt of my past, opening my arms to embrace the chaos.

Only the all-pervading darkness—on the streets, between women's legs, in men's laughter and agents' checkbooks. And the only thing I could turn to was poetry. It was the kind of poetry one couldn't find in textbooks, just an awareness of life on the streets and people's madness, people's self-centered and humbling pursuit of what feels good, and me, in the center of the maelstrom, wondering, blind, aware of the beauty of our madness.

I don't know, maybe I was using the darkness of my existence, that is, the darkness of having no plan for the future, the darkness of living in the present moment only for immediate saturation of my appetites for women, drugs, booze, the party life, the darkness of having nothing to anchor me in the day, nothing to reference me to a meaning that derives from relationships with people—it was as invigorating as it was excruciating.

20.

—

Palabras y luz

AREN'T WORDS, THE USE OF THEM, the whittling and crafting of words and sentences, arranging them to make sense, to convey what my mind and heart yearn to express, isn't that practice supposed to dissolve distances and separations and close the space of misunderstanding between us and get us closer so we can see each other's eyes, and know what feelings flow through them?

If this is true, and I assume it must be since I have devoted my life to the mission, the vocation of rendering the hidden into view, then why have the distances between people, everyday occurrences between people, ignited in hate and hostility so that every day is synonymous with aggression and meanness?

I read the *L.A. Times* today to find wealthy parents cheated on admissions, paying huge amounts of money to get their kids into elite schools. Think Trump here, who warned his college if they released his report card, he'd sue them. Think Trump Jr., think all those wealthy people who paid their way through college and society to get where they are with money—no spirit, no brains, no skill, not anything except money. They hate books. They don't read. Think how dispiriting this is to so many DACA kids holding down three and four jobs to pay their way through school, to mothers holding down three jobs, yearning for an education for their children as the highest goal for living, sweating for slave wages to see their kids graduate.

Think how these wealthy and entitled Pinche Gringos have corrupted that dream with their sleazy lack of ethics.

Yes, it's rigged, in favor of the wealthy whites.

And so I go back to writing. I go back to writing *Working in the Dark*, and read how I was confined to the dungeon below ground for years for wanting to go to school and refusing to work when the warden rejected my plea and I vowed to never work again for the prison system. While these wealthy paper cutouts of people mash the value and spirit of education into the dirt, I lifted it up to set it beside the morning sun.

Most of you know we shouldn't be surprised. You have met enough wealthy people to know they have rotted inside themselves, that the green dollar at some point turned gangrenous and started eating them up with the cancer of greed.

We know that. We also are aware of the fact when we're honest and ethical and work hard to get where we're at, it pays off big in character and spirit and heart—we become beautiful people. And I suppose that's what I feel after all these years, after looking over *Working in the Dark* and writing this new companion book twenty-seven years later, I feel I love myself and am loved and purposeful and balanced and spiritual.

I have it all by virtue of my struggle to educate myself. I am happy with myself as I sit and read "Coming into Language," an essay I wrote in *Working in the Dark*, and I am satisfied twenty years later on a stormy Wednesday morning as I hear that snow is falling at my cabin two hours north of here, pleased with myself that I am still writing and alive.

It could have gone many ways. In my second essay in the book, "Past Present," where I write about going back into prison for the filming of *Blood In/Blood Out* in San Quentin, I never thought I would revisit my old haunt but I almost did, on several occasions during my relapse, return to prison for a long time for possession of drugs.

I was using again. And even as I think back now and wonder how could I ever have used drugs again, how could I chance going back, it shocks me with pain and sadness that I almost did. Everyone has a story: why they fell from grace, why their wives left, their kids hate them, why they turned to the drug of silence and acrimony again. Mine is not different, except that my kids love me, my wife too, that I have a great life and any person with a grain of mindfulness would be happy, and I am, though I don't always appreciate what I have and I fall into the doldrums again and again and risk everything I've worked for, gamble what makes me human for the basest impulses to denigrate myself.

It's a question worth visiting over and over, because if we could ever answer it, there'd be no people like me suffering the lacerations of self-hatred, worthlessness, no self-esteem. Even with all evidence to the contrary, when one is raised homeless and parentless, no matter how many awards and stacks of achievements I am given, that old monster of self-disregard rears its toxic head to sabotage everything.

In "Past Present," I wrote about my inner conflict over acting in a movie where I was once again a convict. I had a breakdown during the shooting and had to be hospitalized for a few days. But I went back out and fulfilled my role as a convict. I knew it well. In many ways, I was still a convict in my heart, and I guess there will always be a part of my heart that has given itself to the convict ways, convict days, convict way of feeling.

This part of my heart is joined by another larger, earlier section of my heart growing up. I remember the despair each evening emitted by the voices of my uncles and mother, a deep timbre of sorrow that evoked the darkness anger inside them and made them fight and create havoc, throw chairs and break each other's bones.

I remember our poverty made me feel like I had inherited the whole world's darkness. That poverty and gossip made us violent. That people talked behind each other's backs and later grew enraged and battled to the death when they saw each other, when they happened to encounter each other in passing. Town against town. Village against village, brother and sister against brother and sister. It was all around me. And that's what the title essay "Working in the Dark" was, about that darkness covering everything, for violence has one power that few other elements in human nature have: it permeates cracks, spaces, long distances, hidden in crevices, the soul's land and the heart's rugged terrain. Violence, once let out, blankets the entire land like the very air we breathe and fills the spaces we inhabit.

If ever there was a mythic fall from innocence, this was it for me: to be born into a place and time and with people who believed violence could purge their pain. It didn't, and it spread over everything and infected everyone. In one way or another, we all got sick and stayed sick for years.

It hides in our memories. And facts mean little to violence, for even if a speck, a granulated molecule embeds itself in your cells, it breeds a cancerous wound that roots into the soul and mind and heart and cannot ever really be extracted or pulled up. And it creates its own story of life through its presence.

It knows what you are going to do, how you will react before you even know; it finds your weakness and laughs at you, it describes you, uses your words to tell about itself while you think you're free of it. What happens to you and your life is a tale often recited by the presence of violence in you. Whatever is told you about violence is a lie, a falsehood, for though on the surface what you are told about yourself seems and sounds like the truth, it is the hidden presence of violence in your bones that is narrating the story. It decides. It is aware far more than you of what you are doing and who you are.

You can, if you're like me, imagine a thousand scenarios for your life in which you leap up into the ethereal lands of goodwill and prosperous adventures, you can summon all your prayers and faith to launch yourself into a life that looks happy, but if you're the child of a violent upbringing, know that it is this that lingers and creeps along the dark spaces in your mind and that it's your ever-present master.

That's the power of violence.

21.

—

Grandma

In my next essay, "Imagine My Life," I recounted how my grandmother always offered me hope and strength. Her life was a symbol of work and perseverance and I wanted mine to be that and I adored her. Yet when I think how she suffered, how strict she was, how impoverished we were, what a harsh life of incredibly spiteful labor did to her, how racism, greed, and selfishness from others really hurt her bad, I remember this and want to lash out at the wealthy white bigots and burn their bank vaults to the ground with all their money inside.

I didn't understand much back then as a kid except that she cut a single tortilla in fours to feed four people. That she mended all the clothes and never bought new shirts or pants, she cared for her house, the linoleum, the walls, the coffee pot, the wood stove, the outhouse, the yard, everything she kept as if it was new because we didn't have money to buy anything else.

I was afraid because I knew how difficult life was for her, I was afraid for myself that somehow I was tied to this merciless life, that I was always going to be a slave for the rich. I was afraid of the white man, afraid to ask for more when I knew he was cheating my grandma, afraid when he snarled at me and called me names, afraid because I knew he had the power to hurt me even worse given the least provocation to do so.

He would starve us. He would jail us. He had the power over us to do whatever he wanted to us and this made me afraid. Even as I reflect on our situation now, I can't help but feel anger at those people who abuse their power.

For so many years I worked at convincing myself not to feel hard toward others who abuse the poor. That's why I love George Lopez, he speaks to that pain in us, he speaks to that darkness, and that's why I loathe the cowards, actors with Latino surnames who have never given as much as a nod in the direction of the barrio, whitewashed sellouts fearful of tainting themselves with our brown *cultura*, using their Hispanic surnames only when its useful to them for a larger payout for their sellout, who do nothing for La Raza, who work only for the dollar, for the white man's pat on the head, to earn a dog biscuit, then retreat to the Hamptons or Martha's Vineyard.

Where have our warriors gone? I know there are warriors standing the line in trenches and they are our scholars, those embattled academics who continue to write papers and essays against all odds, and brilliant they are. Absolutely brilliant. I was nurtured early in my literary life on Ricardo Sanchez, El Tigre, Alurista, J. Chaves, Camarillo, Amiri Baraka, Algarin, Wanda Coleman, Walt Whitman, Allen Ginsberg, Sundiata, Truman Capote, Shakespeare, Quincy Troupe, Gary Soto, Grande, Gloria Anzaldua, Norma Cantú, and many others.

So when I say, "It didn't really hurt me, it didn't hurt, it didn't really, you know, cause me any stress," I am lying. I am trying to cover up my hurt. I am trying to put a smiling face to the wound.

To be honest, I could cry a lot, I could wish for everything that was not and cry for the next ten years because I didn't get what a normal child should expect to get. But instead of the tears rolling down my cheek, I say naw, it's alright, man, didn't really matter.

I look back over my shoulder and see all the kids who died from neglect because racist history books made them hate themselves. I look back and see those bankers who never gave a loan to Chicanos because they didn't trust them and they never got their business off the ground, they were never given even the opportunity to create their dream. A lot of people need to step up and admit you wronged these people. You need to say you're sorry. You need to learn from your mistakes.

22.
—
I Am/Yo soy

In my essay "a look back," from *Working in the Dark*, I talk about going on national reading tours. I think back to the beginning, before my notoriety, when I read at Beyond Baroque in L.A., Libros Revolutionario, and the Living Batch bookstore in Burque, and I am so grateful. Now it's universities, and in those universities I have been boycotted and picketed by Evangelical white supremacists. White supremacists have come out in gangs and mobbed me, white supremacists have thrown stuff at me, have cursed me, have threatened me with violence, because the bottom line is, they don't think a Chicano deserves or has the right to speak on stage.

I feel no qualms about telling those rabble-rousers in the audience to get out, to leave the room until I finish my speech. Then they can come back in, but until then I own the stage.

I could never imagine a future like that for me, but here it is. I am still touring now, going on forty years, universities, conferences, retreats, writing programs, etc., two times a year, and no matter what scenes you decide to conjure up about a convict's life, you better include a man standing on stage and lecturing.

Often I can't believe my good fortune. How did my mestizo people survive? I mean, I should have been dead a long time ago—or never born as pioneers came west spreading plagues, burning and ransacking. How is it I am here?

You have to understand why I respect my ancestors so much, I still can't believe millions of you endured your oppression, but you did and I speak as if a million mouths and tongues and hearts and brains were connected to mine. Though I can no longer see the blood and the agony and the torture, it's there in my soul and I sense it, and I speak now, unafraid and loud, of our truth, the truth that you, somehow, dear ancestors, endured, endured, endured.

I don't have your strength, nor your spiritual faith in God, and the self-love trail's been almost impossible to walk, but over decades, trying to emulate your courage and paying respect to your suffering, I found myself being me again. This morning, sitting here reminiscing over what I wrote twenty years ago in *Working in the Dark*, I find myself now laughing in the light, light emitted from words of love and justice that now illuminate my world, not my path daily but my children's paths as they become doctors and biologists and accountants and filmmakers.

Before my mind takes its lazy detour and snores into its easiest habits of thinking, I must tell you right now, I've met and have befriended the most beautiful and amazing men and women ever to cry at birth.

They have done the work, and somehow—only they know how much they suffered and went through—they came across the bridge and became human beings again and found me and others their equal, people not to be oppressed and hurt and taken advantage of but to lock arms with and share hearts with and be one with our community of humans.

Without them I would have lost all hope. They keep showing up like birds bringing signs of life. They keep imagining the possible and practicing the impossible, burning bridges that separate us, asking us to climb down one side and up the other side, connect through hard work and thoughtfulness, try ways to correct what is wrong, to narrow the pay gap, to get all of us health insurance, to improve the equality of schools, stop racist education, work to clean the environment, be there to show yourself every time a dictator wants to own the air, pollute the earth, give one school new computers and other schools ancient books, be there with your legs and arms and heads and shoulders and heart. Those are the kind of men and women I know.

But imagine, for a second, say you get caught in Mexico, on the border, looking into someone's car, and a policeman suspects you of trying to steal something—an apple, a magazine, a pack of cigarettes—and you're arrested and thrown into a jail cell and later can't make a call or get an attorney and no one pays attention to you, simply forgotten, except by those who harass you and make you do their errands and such. Imagine every single person you meet persecutes you or suspects you of wrongdoing and now you get the idea, little by little, that things are rigged in some manner, that you feel like an outsider, that it doesn't matter whether you're innocent, you're guilty by race—you're white. And you have no room for grievances or excuses or righteous declarations, that fact that you're you is enough to condemn you.

So do you wonder why so many people of color feel like they're living under the duress of white scrutiny? White hypocrisy? It makes you, over years and years, feel like you're already found guilty of whatever they wish to charge you with. Generation after generation you're told by books and people and judges and counselors and neighbors that you're unworthy and inferior. So my suggestion is that when a person of color disdains whites, don't be so quick to judge, understand that her feelings come from an interminable series of bigots and racists and powerful billionaires stripping her of her humanity.

I, for one, am gladdened by imagining a time when there's not an us and them, when there's not a border wall, when there's not people saying I can't speak my language or that my Mexican heritage is offensive. I imagine a time to come when people will love what I do and who I am, that books and songs and TV and movies will reflect this, so that I don't have to keep feeling afraid of every cop I see and every judge and counselor and teacher who seems to believe I am not worth living, that I am taking up space, that I have no right to share the air they breathe.

Yo sé quien yo soy, I know who I am.

(Yesterday, March 15, as I finished writing this piece, the tragic news swept across social media that forty-nine people are dead and forty others wounded in a mass shooting at Christchurch, New Zealand, the shooter, yet another white nationalist terrorist in a long list of white terrorists, Brenton Harrison Tarrant, twenty-eight years old from Australia.)

23.

Swan Dive

In my book *Working in the Dark*, in the essay entitled "La Vida Loca," I describe prison days and go on to tell how I spent my time in diapers in border cantinas my father frequented, where jukeboxes featured Mexican singers wailing corridos. The code of people I was around was more influenced by the heart than by the law, and love simmered among gamblers, outlaws, and prostitutes. *'Chucos* leaned low in plush Caddys, meeting in roadsides and fields and parking lots, where one's manhood was tested and proven in the stories and posture and speech, where candles flickered on altars on cold winter mornings where old men and women knelt and prayed for justice and fair treatment, and where I could feel even as a child that something had been removed from their lives, some absence was present, that made them suffer and squirm under neglect from a larger power towering over them and making them invisible to others.

When my eyes scanned the landscape where I came from and had some morsel of moral obligation to try to even the playing field for others coming behind me, the landscape of injustice and lack of health care and illiteracy ignited in me and took hold in words and I cried out against it.

Years ago my venture into language was innocent and almost fairytale-like: me seventeen working as a custodian in an emergency room in Albuquerque where I often snuck off to the hospital director's office to snooze, where I discovered a book on Chicano resistance and the Chicano Movimiento; then from there another book I stole in the county jail where

I first read Wordsworth, and then borrowing books from prisoners and conscientious Samaritans sending me a dictionary and my writing daily, teaching myself to read and write.

It was romantic, inspiring, almost a sort of epic journey of a chosen child, in Joseph Campbell's myth making and origin creation story—I gave birth to myself.

But now it's different, after decades as a writer, with books and movies and documentaries behind me, published work in almost every genre, and by the grace of God never having sold out to a point where I compromised my ethics and morality away, I stand here at the far side of those early years, filled with gratitude

When I wrote the essay "La Vida Loca," I never dreamed that it would mean poetry has given me more than a full and wonderful life. It's been a buoyant journey, twists and turns, dreadful descents into my worst nightmares, accents blazing with divine radiance into moments of spiritual and emotional and mental clarity, consuming me with a grounded certainty in the goodness of life that was strong enough, this feeling of elation that words and poems and books offered me, strong enough to carry the burden of any grief or societal catastrophe or crisis.

Language marked me as its warrior and implemented its design on my psyche, even though it was never clear to me what that design was. Blindly groping at hope, I went forth into the war zones of injustice and literary bias and educational racism and spoke what I felt was my truth, spoke, that is, plagued with all my flaws and faults and moral dilemmas. I didn't squeak away like a mouse to some bureaucratic position in the mayor's administration, nourishing secret desires to one day have power and be a politician. It takes balls to be a poet, it's the toughest game in town. And I thank God for the unrivaled and immeasurable meaning and purpose it gave me.

24.

On Being in Joy's Embrace

THE CONTRADICTIONS ARE TOO VAST THESE DAYS to make any sense, too many outrageous crimes against human nature committed alongside the blasé, the common, the banal, all swirling around us like some kaleidoscope hallucination, so dizzying, sometimes it's just too much.

Where are the groundings? I glance at my essay "Groundings," in *Working in the Dark*, and I smile at its innocence, the fervor and righteous attitude of its writer, the opening of his heart as if begging alms of the ocean. I wrote that I had finished a poetry reading tour with a dozen universities and returned to Los Angeles to continue my career as a screenwriter and filmmaker, and I went to the ocean and sat on the sand.

I was so naïve and romantic back then, and in the twenty years that have passed there has been so much joy and confusion and mistakes and sorrow. So much of life's debris, its cataclysmic wreckage swept out to the sea of memory, out there somewhere absorbed by time that seems like a street sweeper each morning, pushing its broom of who we were yesterday and what we did, our thoughts and emotions and what our eyes saw and hands touched and ears heard, all pushed before the street sweeper's broom.

It's hard to remember things distinctly. The ocean is a great leveler. It whispers to the shores, "Live your life, live your life."

I look at my notes this morning. I seem to be preoccupied with injustice these days. I wrote this, "The snow is a foot deep outside. How many homeless are freezing tonight, how many have no jobs? A criminal con man scurries about the White House, bent on destroying our beautiful planet, its animals and plants, climate change threatens our existence, children are dying in camps at our southern borders, many writers have silenced themselves, deciding to opt out of the social dialogue and dissident activism, and become press-release versions of cheerleaders in the stands, eating popcorn and drinking Cokes."

Every morning I wake up to more and more crises everywhere I read. And no matter how much I think of ways to lessen my anxiety, it increases. I worry about my kids' future. About people. About America.

To be honest with you, the asylum seekers often make me smile when we're working or talking on a project. Their comments are tinged with the dried-blood edge that things can always get worse and one must appreciate the moment, even if it's brought tears to your eyes and pain to your heart, enjoy the sense of being present.

Not like those Buddhist monasteries full of trust-funders smiling that kind of bumper-sticker smile: no, the asylum seekers offer the smile that knows hunger and service and penance and suffering. And their self-effacement always manages to make me feel happy and believe for a second that we as a species might have a chance to survive our own stupidity.

In "Groundings" I write about our impermanence, how everything just goes by, diminished with time into air. Except for the voice of the ocean, whispering our ludicrous self-inflated importance. Laughing at us.

I write about my lust for living, about the journey, and this is where any reasoning breaks down—it's all too much, this life, this heavy abundance of pleasures and experience and stimulation and sightings, too much. I guess one must turn to God for any rest, for the mind to ooze back into its quiet reverie of unquestioning acceptance of the way things are. And that's what is difficult if not impossible for me.

I love rallying out into the battlefield with a cry that rattles even hell's cell bars and wakens the devil to leap back and cower in a corner. Too much life in me, too much love, too much beauty, too many beautiful nights and dawns have kissed and licked and loved me back.

I have been infected by the canyons in New Mexico, the sunlight, the prairies and horses and dogs, the hawks and lizards and roadrunners. Sometimes at five or six or seven I'll get out of bed and cry. Sometimes on a winter morning or a sun-blistered dawn, I'll come out and wish so hard to return to my childhood, I can hear in my rib cage a great orchestra strumming its theme song for a movie where life is again heroic and sublime and courageous.

25.
—

Fulfillment

In my essay "creativity," I write how I feel like I finally won something in life. I won a small, cellular speck of elation, that's what I feel when I write, when I am creative, I feel in the flow of gravity and time, part of the microcosmic undulations of matter flowing invisible. I feel myself being put together again, being pieced together, thread by thread, string by string, radiant with life and glowing with light.

This has nothing to do with ambition to scale the lofty heights of a career. What an inexperienced young man I was at thirty, ill-prepared and lacking any planning at all to enter the golden halls of academia and Hollywood, and I guess in some way that explains our existence. In the end, our life is about how we show up unprepared, how we come ill-prepared to meet our fate, and we end up some years down the road in a room with a blue blanket covering our bed, sunlight pouring through the window, listening to a song that fills our hearts with remorse for what we failed at and joy that we were chosen. Such sadness is beautiful because it shows our innocent fragility and our vulnerability.

The kitchens, the meals, the textbooks and the teachers, the friends, the nights we watched movies, the envelopes that arrived with checks to get us by, all of it slides away, leaving a plate with a half-eaten cookie, and sleeping children in the bedrooms, while I sit awake like a miracle happening and unfolding second by second, making me part of an esteemed fellowship of poets and writers all over the world.

Many have given their lives, like the hundreds of journalists murdered in Mexico by government and gangsters and criminals. They wrote the truth and I am part of that legacy and so honored to be a brother of Gerard Manley Hopkins, Emily Dickinson, and countless others. I am family to the editors in New York, the publishers in Chicago, the journalists in Detroit, the poets in L.A., and my family stretches and expands globally to those dissidents and brave poets in prison in Russia and North Korea for writing poetry, those executed for writing, those in Brazil murdered, those everywhere, Saudi Arabia where poets and writers are beheaded. Being part of this bloodline, this spirit-line, makes me feel blessed and obliged to do the best I can, and I try, often not making the mark these persecuted poets and writers live by. But I try.

No, I was not one of those who took the road less traveled, but maybe, at my best, I took the curves less traveled, the small wildlife path across a field less traveled, maybe a quarter mile, a city block, or even a few feet less traveled.

I am not as strong as many poets, but I feel safe and nurtured and intimate as a brother to those courageous poets and writers out there right now, rising to edit, to fiddle with lines, to write in their belief and doubt that they have anything worthy to say but still they insist on trying because they have people to praise, distances to explore, spirits to develop and expand— and so they rise and write and wash and go hungry and worry about bills and keep stepping forward, for all of us. Their words are torches in the dark for the rest of us too frail to attempt the work.

Thank you all, from coast to coast, on every continent, mountaintop to valley, hovel and palace, male and female, thank you, mil gracias compañeras y caballeros. Thank you for offering me your hand and lifting me up, thank you for the kind words you write, thank you for your empathy and militancy, for your awareness, your knowledge, your constantly making yourself count, for standing the line, *gracias*! On behalf of my grandparents and community and society, thank you.

26.
—
Poet and Reader Relationships

I COULD HAVE EASILY BEEN DISMISSED. But you didn't let that happen. On evenings when I walked alone in the prison compound, when I wondered how to be a good father, when the setting sun seemed to tell me that life is sad and silent and that I was no more than a mere speck in it, you didn't let it happen. You loved reading my poems. You empathized with me, homeless kid, parentless man, someone who rose from the embers and ashes and bones of a life to become a poet, you came from out of the darkness, a traveler, and sat at my fire and warmed your hands and said you loved me. A stranger, your eyes reckoned time, almost like a god who knew me, who knew all my days, who accepted me, my naïvety, my innocence, my pride, my arrogance meant little to you for you felt the sorrow running beneath my words, my facial expressions, my features, you knew that beneath all my bravado there was a frightened child seeking to hold someone's hand to guide me out from my wilderness.

So from the essay titled "Creativity," I write another one called "Pushing Through," and I talk about the orphanage, and I recognize I am still the small boy using metaphor to conceal my truth because I haven't fully thought out my innocence, how to say it, write it, cry it, and laugh it in words.

I can now speak my truth. Despite all the clamor by the righteous in our society, I know that it is wrong to use the most advanced and sophisticated military against citizens in Gaza using sticks and stones. I know it is wrong to oppress them, starve them, treat them worse than cattle, brand them, imprison women and children, so many wounded, missing limbs, while the Israelis dine at open air cafés and laugh and keep expanding their rule, taking wantonly what they want, disregarding international censure, they don't care; I know it's wrong to label asylum seekers criminals and the ludicrous charge by a madman that starving children are invading America—it's beyond deserving of any commentary, you must be insane to believe that or riddled so deeply with fear and paranoia that you need to be sheltered in an asylum yourself; I know it's wrong to imprison so many young men and women for crimes to the rich and get richer, I know it's wrong the justice system gives no quarter to Chicanos or brown people, because we have no money to purchase justice; I know it's wrong when I see the poverty and crumbling schools, when I see old people dying from lack of insurance, I know it's wrong and I can attest to it, in my poetry and in my day-to-day life.

You cannot ever make me believe that destroying women and children and innocent men is right.

Ever.

And you allowed me, dear reader, to say my piece, why? Because this is America, because my rights to free speech are protected. As a Chicano, my words deal with being a Chicano, and come to you from *Working in the Dark* by the titles of the essays "A View from the Other Side" and "Q-Vo" and "¿De Quiéncentennial? Puro Pedo. . . " and "L.A., Ése. . . ," and years later in this second volume of essays, *Laughing in the Light*, because Chicano is not simply a historical label, nor a cultural or spiritual designation, the word *Chicano* embeds itself in the cellular fabric of my being, it's part of the molecule and DNA of my spirit, and if we could define God, what he looks like, what he eats for breakfast, does he run, do push-ups, how does he dress, does he swim, does he speak Caló, well, then, I could describe Chicano and what it means to me.

One thing for certain, what I write is undergirded with Chicano sensibility and that language is permeated and fused into my heart's beating Chi-Chicano, Chi-Chicano . . . beating with words, because before language, I could have been the kid with his brains scattered over the wall from a bullet behind my head, the kid stabbed on the street corner, the kid tied to a pillar by the police in a basement in the open where cops passing by could mock and jeer at him. But once I called myself Chicano I was a leader of society, I was a decision maker, I was a kind and loving man, I was captain of my destiny and great husband and lover, and I was the guiding light for my children.

Once my tongue dipped its tip into the holy nectar of the Word, my Chicanismo came alive, I felt baptized, saw heavenly light shooting its rays from the rooftops of words, sliding down the walls of words, and then I saw Jesus walking toward me on the air, his beautiful bronze skin, his robes, his long curly black hair, and he says, "Q-Vo Santiago"; when words roll on my tongue, like a hummingbird with Chicano eyes and wings, the world fills with flowers, petals, blossoms, and at each day's end, I fall into bed tired from the nectar and the abundance of beauty all around me. My memories shot up in me and I felt like Spider-Man, shooting length of webs from memory to memory, scaling impossible depths of time and covering great spaces from place to place.

And then words birth my unformed self into being, into its Coming, where I find myself laughing in the light, so much light blinds me as if every violin found its owner's hands and fingers and they all decided to play a nostalgic song to what was, what is, what will be, and from the strings words float up and away, just-born orange monarch butterflies, and on the air describe what you are feeling, strumming with a power of joy kids feel when they fit their first baseball glove on, or climb up to their first tree house—a poor man waiting for months for his first iPhone, when Black Friday arrives, he's first at Walmart's doors, and see him barrel his way through the unruly mob, bull-rush down anyone to get to the electronics department. In his joy to own his first iPhone what does he do? Call his daughter, his son, his wife.

That's how it was for me learning to read and falling in love with books and like all love affairs, after the initial elixir, the brooding sets in from betrayals and false expectations and in this case, it was when I read about the Quincentennial bullshit of America being discovered by Europeans. I was like what? I was discovered? When? Weren't we always here, didn't we have our societies and tribes long before any colonial scammer set his greedy foot on our shores? What's this about being discovered?

And I encounter the same drivel in tourist brochures over and over— for example, when I read that Georgia O'Keeffe called Cerro Pedernal her mesa because she painted a picture of it. And her painting is reproduced on postcards all over the world and now people arrive asking, "Where's O'Keeffe's mountain?"

Talk about revising history. (Almost as disappointing as white writers who make a lucrative living writing detective stories as if they're Navajo.)

We're going to dismiss a hundred years of tribal affiliation with it, we're going to eliminate all those people before who claimed it as their religious refuge, we're going to blind ourselves to those indigenous people who found redemption in it, who lived there (and still do in Abiquiú), who honored it, who followed their lineage of generations before them, and now, it suddenly belongs and was discovered by this old white lady?

Kidding me?

That's when I realized we needed more truthful writers and historians. That's when all these parades and patriotic fevers shocked me. I thought they were just having fun, but after reading about it, I realized they were celebrating discovery of me and my land.

So my Chicanismo unfolded its wings for a full-glide flight, and I wrote about the 1492 myth makers, who should have stayed in their mother's kitchens making cupcakes and not sat at a desk writing fantasy history.

A certain panic clutched my mind because I thought, in horror, that every schoolchild of color was reading this. That these historians were stealing the truth from our children's inheritance and replacing it with white superiority lies.

When I first read it, it took me weeks to get over the fact that school allowed and fostered these delusions. I dug deeper and found out that there was indeed a healthy battalion of Chicano/a academics doing amazing research and writing, challenging those colonial, myopic views (just that the publishers were not distributing their work).

They persist, however, and we have our writers and poets and fiction writers publishing in dozens of languages and on best-seller lists and speaking and lecturing on our history all over the world. They're not only breaking new ground, but smashing the myth of unlimited opportunity for minorities, stripping the blinders from gullible assumptions that there is no racism—the castle of this fairytale of white superiority is crumbling fast into a pile of rubble and wasteland debris of what was and is replaced by indigenous truth.

To believe they discovered Cerro Pedernal and that O'Keeffe named it hers, as if it hadn't had a name before in a dozen Native languages, is to believe the giant, gray-bearded man in red woolies can really slide down a chimney.

Cerro Pedernal is part of our creation story, as is the Rio Grande and every arroyo and mesa in New Mexico, and just because you're a rich white lady doesn't mean you can go around New Mexico renaming our historical sites and villages claiming to have discovered this and that because you paint it. Long before your brushes etched color on white canvas, many tribes had painted it on their flesh, parleyed with it in dreams and visions, wrote on buffalo skins, on rocks.

It's a case of cultural appropriation and we know it all too well here in New Mexico.

Inherent in my Chicanismo, this love for my raza, is the need to set the record straight. Dozens of poets in New Mexico countered the Quincentennial clamor with poetry readings in coffee shops and bookstores, denouncing the fabrication of American history, filled as it was with European soupy noodles and purple meatballs (Columbus's favorite meal).

And when it was my turn to read poetry, I filled classrooms with the beauty of my Mexican grandpa, my India Mexican grandma, my Mexican *tíos* and *tías,* and my Chicano heart and reciting a kind of poetry that made my little brothers and sisters smile because it reflected our love for our *gente* and *la tierra*. And when those students got older and went to college, they taught their professors about our history, and they continue to raise their hands in their classrooms to educate teachers about who they are.

They use words and phrases like *chale, la onda, q-vo, a la ve*, and soon even campus posters are celebrating our cultural treasures, our Chicano moratorium, commemorating our treaties and language.

No longer are we sold textbook snake oil for the wound of oppression. No longer do our children sit at a desk as if it were a prison cell, no longer are we failed for having pride and love for our Chicano ancestry, and no longer do they send us to the principal or expel us for trying to reason and educate them.

Our young men and women, they know, as I learned, that language was a power where our sadness and grief could be understood, and while words didn't teach you to accept or endure the pain of racism, they did allow an outlet for a response to it.

Don't ever give a kid the power to speak his heart because when you do, idols of authority start to crumble. Learn to wear a hardhat. Get some heavy welder's gloves cuz it's going to get hot. Learn to duck, move fast, cry when it's inappropriate, and for god's sake, don't appropriate what's not yours.

Once you control the narrative, the story of your love for your people, you'll find others want to get in behind it and claim it as theirs, say they're you, vow they've been oppressed as you have and they know what it is to be confined behind bars for twenty-five years, they'll tell you that.

But don't get pissed. You're living it, they're talking it, you're suffering and celebrating it, they're wishing and fantasizing it. Even, be forgiving and understanding but unafraid to tell them they're wrong. It's not as easy as that, to say you're me. You're not. And that's good. The more variety of people, the merrier the assemblage of amazing people we find ourselves to be.

It's so insane, isn't it, that we have celebrities who live from diaper change to champagne brunch going on national media to express their solidarity with people who have been the victims of oppression and injustice? Isn't it insane that there are those who denounce you if you write a poem about Palestinian children getting slaughtered weekly by Israeli military? They label you anti-Semite when really all you are is a compassionate human being witnessing the truth.

27.
—

L.A., después . . .

L.A., HOW I LOVE YOU, much like a hot day in summer, like a hawk circling a cliff, like a palm tree, like a breeze, like a girlfriend I love and love but who is never home when I come knocking on your door. A green door with a brass knocker. The door handle rubbed raw to its undercoat and to bare metal by many desperate hands and palms dreaming of being actors, dreaming of stages, of cameras, of fame and power and love and wealth.

My sweet L.A., there's always strangers living with you. What do I have to give you, what offerings might you like, what can I lay at your feet so you might bestow your blessings on me?

How about a Chicano homage? So many of us leave home on a pilgrimage to your shores, we leave family and lovers, to arrive later and say, "L.A., *Ése*" (as my essay is titled in *Working in the Dark*), L.A., Ése, we greet you like a lost friend, we parted at our last fight but now enough time has passed so we realize we miss and love each other.

L.A. Ése, come, bring me your prostitutes—all those men and women giving up ass and pussy for a shot at fame, bring me your whores, all those men and women willing to do anything for a scabby, virus-infected producer to get a small part in a movie, L.A. Ése, bring them to me so I might kiss and hug and feed them, shelter them in my words and praise them for their dreaming. And we will wait out the winters and summers together, sitting on the beach watching the waves play with the moon and sunrise, we will sit there and wait on our ship that we believe makes its way to our shore.

That's what language does. It makes you confront your assumptions, it makes you bear witness, it strums its guitar strings and waits for you to sing your truth knowing there will be those waiting with blades in the shadows ready to cut your tongue out and silence you.

But for us boys and girls reared on hunger, we don't scare all that easy. We were not brought up to surrender, we have too much love for parents, for our gente. We will out-wait our enemies. We will be here during the coldest days and hottest noons, you'll see us, thirty or forty million of us Latinos, in line to vote, filling classrooms, graduating, we go nowhere, we rise from the earth of our ancestors, and we walk it, we love it, we honor it.

And as my essay "Making Do—Chicano Style" says, if you give us hunger, we'll make do. If you give us poverty, we'll make do. We will make do with whatever neglect you try to punish us with, because we are magicians of adapting to any situation, and once we learn to use words as I have to express my feelings, we become a power that is unassailable, and we cannot be conquered.

I sit and write this, and I still use words to express my ideas. Not a gun. Not my fist. Not hatred. I think in images, in feelings, and depend on the propulsion of feelings to drive me through a paragraph, sentence to sentence, with my emotions afire, flaring like a volcano erupting at night.

As I begin to acquire the skill to articulate myself, as I understand what other writers penned, amazed and often in wonder as I quietly repeat their lines, their images, their ideas, often their beauty and impact leave me in silence, laughing in their light, bathed in their radiance.

But I didn't have the confidence nor the ability to utter such profound words. I hid behind my metaphors, words were my sword and knight's chain mail, my shields, my protection against exposure that might submit me to shame or even worse, censure.

This appointment will not be canceled. I will not vanish, I will not be intimidated. Now, twenty years after writing *Working in the Dark* and looking back, I smile at the naïve young man I was. I fly across the years and embrace him, there in a house in L.A. writing screenplays, enjoying one-nighters, hanging out at the farmer's market drinking morning coffee in the minty air, the salty brine of sand and waves in the breeze; not understanding how fortunate I was, how fateful it turned out that I was sitting in the passenger seats of some of the most creative directors in the world, and how I didn't do anything but read poetry and write essays and never once (which shocks me) did I dream of a career in Hollywood.

I tried the genre of screenwriting and loved it and vowed I would be back to write more features, but I left to follow my love for poetry. And so, after a couple of features, I came home to pursue a life of writing poetry, raising hell, got divorced and became homeless, starting using coke again and hanging out with the losers, the whores and addicts and sluts, and I was intent and willful as a fish who just snapped a fishing line.

I swam on, flashing my tail and fins upstream to mate with God again and again, to drink and use, anything to lose myself in dissolution. Rather than face my emptiness and get serious and get real with myself, I opted for more drugs and booze and women to numb myself.

And that beautiful man I was should have long ago been mashed under God's heel into a sidewalk smudge, but I was spared by a forgiving angel, given a reprieve, and Quetzalcoatl and Tonantzin's merciful hands touched my head and said, "Live, you fool, live and prosper for your daughter, your sons, your loyal and beautiful new love in your life, Stacy, for all of us, live."

And so here we are, me at 5 a.m., reading news of asylum seekers, DACA students, refugees crowding the southern border, and our one and only Orange Haired Clown himself perpetuating white nationalism—what a fool, and what idiots we are to have such a fool directing global traffic. I sense a cataclysmic traffic jam coming. Who could have imagined such a country, a carnival house of mirrors? Such a trouncing of our democracy?

Ah, well, Americans have and will go on in the midst of this turmoil and madness. Democracy teaches us to live with our mistakes, and I go back to these essays and realize I could have made better decisions. I don't regret the ones I made, but somehow I sense a deeper drumbeat was calling me forth into the areas of human experience that had nothing to do with power, wealth, or entitlement—my goal was to live and enjoy and suffer and hopefully learn from what I did.

And what a journey it has been.

So many opportunities! I recall a particular famous actor wanted to buy my screenplay. I tried to sell it to him earlier, but he lowballed me so bad it verged on an insult and then when I sold it to Hollywood Pictures he went into a tailspin and you'd think he had ants in his pants. Everybody was aghast that I said no to him. He kept playing the race card, saying, "Well, if you were a real Chicano you'd give it to me." And, "You're a sellout selling it to a gringo director," and stuff like that. Something about Hollywood reminds me of a leaky bedpan filled with a patient's excrement and urine. It smells.

One hears so many sad stories from wealthy writers, especially the ones suffering from Napoleon's small-size syndrome—that is, they came hoping to make enough money writing so they could then write the book they really want to write—about their father in New York, about a lost love, about blah blah blah. In the end, no matter what came out of their mouths, they set aside the story that drove their hearts to want to be writers, and opted for the money, and screw their original commitment. The money's too good, and who can blame them?

I didn't go for this famous actor's subtle denigration of my character and motivation, I knew what I did and why I did it, but now, on the rebound, suddenly he loves me, he wants to buy my screenplay and if I let him, then I'm a Chicano. Wow, big surprise.

I didn't sell it to him, of course, and therein started a rumor that I was heartless, a sellout, no good, that I couldn't be trusted, that I was in the enemy's camp, that I was a Judas. I never told anyone about the fact that I offered it to him first and he turned me down.

But in Hollywood, when an actor is famous, it's almost as if he is untouchable, on the level of saints and popes. There's a certain adulation that develops among other actors, as if the actor who landed a great role that's going to make him famous and rich is in tune with the divine spirits of the universe and he can, if you worship him devoutly and kiss his fingers, bring you happiness and fulfillment. Honestly, I've never experienced such a bedpan of mishmash. It stinks.

Perhaps, as some would argue, I entered the arena of life ill-prepared for life's wise choices, always needing to butt my head against obstacles, filled with awe and wonder and innocence at a tree or sunrise or ocean wave and not a speck of outsmarting my fellow human beings engrained in my being.

I was smooth as water calling out to the thirst of life, filling its gourd with my soul, pouring it to the brim to slake its thirst. I didn't worry about money, though I was broke most of the time, I didn't worry about friends, though I yearned for them, I didn't worry about this ridiculous thing called career where one gives his whole life to a corporation, I didn't worry about my health, nothing, except the next poem, the next book, the next person I met, I lived entirely in the moment, utterly mindless of tomorrow. Enjoying today's promise filled with unknown turns and curves and shadows and all-blinding light.

I know I leave myself open to easy criticism, I make the unpopular choices and say things that are politically incorrect. And not for one second should you think that I was not treated with kid gloves, that everyone I met at the hundreds of universities where I read or conferences I keynoted welcomed me with open hearts and love, yes, love. The magic happened and continues to happen.

My poetry takes me and my readers to a communal region in the great heart of the universe, and there we share, relate, discuss, listen; there we meet somewhere outside ourselves, above us, we join. I came, we met in a third person and we danced as we hugged our souls wrapping around each other into a spiritual toga, one shroud as holy as the Nazarene's and as bloody as Caesar's robe—love and betrayal, mixed properly, consummate in the highest honor a human soul can experience.

I really did enjoy (and continue to) the standing-room crowds and dinners and signing of books like no other writer, I suspect, because being an ex-con, a kid with no family, a poet with no societal upbringing, how to explain the grace and munificence of people who opened their hearts and minds for me and brought me into their hearts? I mean, really, not many humans can say as much, and I had this miracle of love over and over. One thing for certain, no one can ever predict or tell the future when it comes to how people will act—in my case, I flowered into a million blossoms cascading over L.A. like bougainvillea in a summer ocean morning breeze. Change is always in the air.

28.
—
Political Poet

It takes a long time to know the book business, to get into it in a good way. Too many times I wrapped myself around what a poet was supposed to be like, too many times I imagined what a writer should do and it was all wrong. The book business, that is, the mission and life of a writer, is like any other profession except it gets personal, it gets to be you in the world canoeing over waterfalls to find some immortal truth about your being and it often happens in sizzling ways, it often happens in surprising and life-fulfilling ways, and it's a beautiful thing. That's perhaps why I couldn't grasp the book business and that's why many writers are so successful early on: they know the game, they send the thank-you cards, they don't get drunk and crazy when they read, they're sweet, predictable pawns—I never was.

An abundance of passion was my problem, thinking that writing was also the business of priesthood, I was a priest, some voodoo word enchanter living in the backwoods and getting high and drinking and having sex and mixing it all up to give the brew the name poet.

I came into the publishing world with a defiant attitude toward literary foundations and then after a long time, after witnessing their work, how they distribute books to so many poor people caught up in housing projects and reservations and barrios, how they advocate building libraries and enhancing curriculums with diversity, I grew to respect and love them.

There was a time when I thought being a poet meant forsaking all help, never reaching out, being distant and outlawish, but I had it all wrong—I should have accepted the outstretched hand they offered but I simply didn't know. I wasn't ready to accept kindness, to be recognized and loved and cherished, and they were. I had some growing to do.

I had to get rid of my fear of rejection. Humble myself.

I had to step back and make my peace with the publishing world and other writers. I wasn't one of them, I was the outsider, I didn't know how to tell them I was an odd one, that I wasn't going to be able to walk in those shoes, that I was all wrong for the job. But they didn't go for it, they loved me and they had faith that I'd come around or die trying and I was willing to go to any extent and degree or distance to cross that bridge where I was okay being me as writer/poet.

I did it.

And I was proud of myself. I was getting better at getting along with people—granted, not as good as those writers and poets who grow up creating friendships with literary people and philanthropists in all the right places and when it comes time for prizes, they're on the tongue tips of all of the judges because they've cultivated them, learned how to be one of them, how to acquire their tastes, how to exist in their universe.

Not me, I was born a wild little snot-nosed kid running the prairie and that's probably where I'll end up, I love the wind too much, I love the dirt roads, love the silence that fills the air, the quiet in the prairie blossom, the mountains, and the people who live in vast spaces of silence for long periods of time. Their silence is a season all its own and tells of the springs that the soul enjoys and the wintry absences of warmth.

When you start getting a whiff of southern literature, then New York and Jersey writers' work, and thinking there's a chance you might be a part of this amazing legacy, this ancestral copal fire burning at the pyramid's point of a pencil writing words to narrate a poem, then it just blows you away and you try, like I did, to take one step forward toward the outstretched arms of a poet or philanthropist and learn, like a toddler, how to walk again in trusting those people.

It feels so good to come back, where I'm writing this now, in NOLA, where I'm visiting Tulane for the National Book Foundation, and the reason it does is that I used to drive through here when I was a teenager, hauling hundreds of pounds of weed, bound for Georgia and North Carolina, here's where I first saw the aboveground burial sites, and how I loved those days, how I love second chances at trying to get it right, how I love forgiveness, how that is the only reason I'm here I believe, 'cause there's a lot of folks out there who never gave up on me.

I loved my publisher at New Directions. Griselda Ohannessian. One in a million. I regret not spending more time talking with her. If only we had more like her, fewer business-minded editors and more poetry lovers, I think literature in general would benefit. I'm sure readers would be happy. But, alas, not to be—the great publishing machine wheels crank forth, ripping the bones from its joints in the old publishing style, synthesizing the ripped limbs from the torso and reassembling the industry in a more mechanized efficient manner that attends to its marketing strategies.

I think of Griselda as I look over my book of essays *Working in the Dark*, written at a time when I'd go to New York and drop by the New Directions Publishing office to see her, stand out on the balcony, and as we gazed out at the buildings, we'd smoke a cigarette and talk. I remember her saying one time, "You did it, Jimmy."

And I know she meant that I had accomplished quite a lot, in poetry and also, at that particular time, with a feature film by Hollywood Pictures taking the Big Apple by storm, long lines curved around blocks, I read at MOMA, at bookstores, on stages. It was a fun time, a wild time.

And now, years later, as I sift through the essays and notice they're mostly about who I am, where I come from, my Chicano gente and raza blues, the culture and injustice and the love we have, the *cora*, as we call that fierce love, that leaves no room for questioning, no room for surrender, no room for doubt—it moves as the tiger moves, forward, bared fangs and flared claws.

It would have been so much easier to write a thriller, a fishing story, a hunting epic, instead of focusing on poetry and my culture. I wrote about me as if I was an outlaw I followed. I wrote about me the way a journalist writes about a folk hero and I'm puzzled why these essays deal so much with the philosophy of who we are; why did I take to myself like an unknown character and draw out my ideas and feelings and anger and loves, why was I the character of study, why? It would have been so much easier to create a story about a village fighting for water rights against a corporation—we have so many here in New Mexico that come in and ravage the land.

But instead, I write about change. About my dreams for a better life. Which hasn't changed. My brother, my parents, my imprisonment, my kids, about the beauty of the land. I write about language, how each word is a crystal, placed in a certain position, collecting the earth's vibrational energy and emitting electric light, a radiance, a deeper understanding than mere logic or reason, and spilling over into subconscious metaphor and symbol to explain one's sorrow or joy.

That hasn't changed.

Some folks just have to jump up in your face and BE HEARD. And cowards do that by taking automatic weapons to grade schools and murdering innocent children. Big heroes.

Then you have the flip side of the coin: I remember speaking to a large audience at Berkeley. I was reading my poem "Rita Falling from the Sky," about a Raramui woman who killed her husband and then walked from Chihuahua to Kansas and was imprisoned in a Kansas hospital for the insane for decades. As I was reading, a woman at the back of the auditorium stood up and cried, "I am Rita. I am Rita."

I looked to see a middle-aged white woman, raising her fist and pumping it, as if she wanted to get a crowd chant going. And she might have had I not interjected, "No, my dear, you are not Rita."

I would agree that to some degree white women have been oppressed— gender-based discrimination catches all who are not old white men in its razor-wire net—but the system has been rigged in their favor for a long time.

White is the color advertisers and politicians aspired to for a long time. But when it comes to social inequities, as shown by the #metoo movement, white women petition the courts and get money, are listened to, empathized with, and generally either get a movie role or a fat check for being offended and short-changed. I've yet to see an immigrant or asylum seeker, after being raped by guards and gangs, get anything but a kick in the ass and tossed back into the lion's den where thieves and guards and ICE can rape them with immunity.

So don't tell me you're Rita. I'm speaking of a day-to-day and hour-by-hour oppression that follows a woman of color, about the million tiny seconds that are like blades that assail a woman of color on a bus, washing dishes, cleaning toilets, at school, everywhere.

Still, even writers try their hand at confessing with all due decorum that they are as badly off and as belittled and neglected as a woman of color: take *Hillbilly Elegy* or *Educated*, both by writers who present themselves as seriously disadvantaged and write about their misery and poverty and violence and how they scaled the gleaming halls of academia to become lawyers and professors. Take the Cormac McCarthy novels, his western sagas about how white men slaughter every Native they encounter to settle the West despite tremendous hardship. His heroes are white serial killers. Publishers love to feed this kind of tripe to readers because it assuages white guilt, gets them to thinking and feeling about southern black slaves or the southwestern Mexican and the Natives, who were buried under the hooves and bullets of the cavalry and foot soldiers and then robbed of everything, life, future, you name it. The system concocted by racists and white domestic terrorists took all it could from people of color, and now we have poor-me books asking for pity and commiseration because they were treated unfairly.

Admission of guilt and accountability come first, before any reckoning and alliance and friendship. And forgiveness. History is a cruel judge and sooner or later demands that the truth be unveiled and given space to speak.

I was not so conscious of racism or injustice when I first started publishing my poems, coming into the poetry world and meeting so many nice editors and publishers and other poets. I felt certain I had found my place in the world. That I needn't look further, this was what I wanted to do in life. It promised me so much and only asked that I live, that I experience, that I be fearless in searching my heart, that I not clam up and corrupt the process.

Join in, along with thousands of others from all corners of the earth and make your words sing, make them praise the hardworking men and women and seasons and seasonal gristle of life.

As Dylan Thomas wrote, "Do not go gentle into that good night," and I didn't.

There are some things that just don't seem to make any sense, like accusing the migrants and mothers and children who come to America seeking asylum from murderous drug lords and American-installed dictators of being terrorists and drug kingpins, when in fact very few have been proven to be so. No, instead, most terrorists and drug kingpins are white, American-born males and I guess the reason the far right-wing conservatives insist on perpetrating this lie is to disguise their racism.

A brief look into America's past is telling. All whites are immigrants, they came here fleeing persecution or poverty and many were downright coming to grab what they could by any means necessary. They were con artists, scammers, liars, and criminals. Of course, history has dressed them up as courageous folk heroes, the Davy Crlocketts and Paul Bunyans and John Waynes, good ol' boys sent by God to settle the land and civilize the savages. Historians in those days were all white. Many had never met a Native and knew little about our customs. You see the same thing happening today with Muslims: we demonize them so we can persecute them. Same thing happened with Indians.

But white nationalists were also assisted in their lies by the knee-benders, the fort Indians, the sweet Mexican girl with flowers in her hair, unwilling to raise her voice in anger. History mocked us, described us as sweet little sombrero-in-hand illiterates.

Still, seems like the time to fess up has come: White nationalists are scared, and a good deal of that fear comes from the truth, from journalists and poets of color writing history from their point of view, from the truth of their experience, and the facts as they happen, adding those facts to the social tragedies of today, undermining the malcontented mind seeking to own and run and have all the power over others and accumulate vast sums of wealth to subjugate poor, hardworking Americans.

And now they want to stop immigrants coming to America so they can continue their unbridled entitlement and leisurely existence. That's the definition of a coward.

They want to keep America white, and if that means accusing Jesus himself of criminal underworld racketeering, I have no doubt they'll try. It might be time, and I suggest this also for Republicans and Democrats too, to repeat the Serenity Prayer out loud every hour, God grant me the serenity to accept . . . when you're addicted to power and wealth and the good-old-boy system of getting all the government contracts, it's probably time for intervention and that's what I think poets are doing today, finally, becoming unafraid of being political in their work.

29.

—

The Unbelievable Naïvety of My Friend Pancho

I PROMISED MYSELF I would never set foot in another prison after we finished filming *Blood In/Blood Out* and left San Quentin. And even though I got offers to write other screenplays and even act in several movies, I'd had enough of Hollywood and decided to return to Albuquerque and go back to writing my poetry and reading.

It was a simple life but one that filled me with wholesome purpose. I figured I was going to live my life by my terms—not pursuing money, not going after academic positions (though I got offered several), not sacrificing the only life I had by surrendering my dreams to someone else's ambitions, no. The poem's magic had me for life, as if poetry were a divine prophecy I designed my life around. Movies, Hollywood, matinee stars, and luxury and enormous payouts, I could do without. I wanted my life back.

I didn't stay true to my promise for long, however. I am not going to go over all the misery of my past experiences confined by the American Correction Department. If you want to delve into it, read *A Place to Stand* or *Working in the Dark*. You'll get a good dose of where I'm coming from.

My promise of never going back was broken by a Chicano convict draped in chains. He confronted me one cold winter morning when I was invited to give a talk at a certain prison and he said I only came for the check—it was a big one—and I admitted to him yes, that's why I'm here.

But that evening, back in the motel, I couldn't sleep, and the next morning I went back to the prison and asked the warden if I could come back and facilitate a writing workshop, which I did for the next nine months. That was thirty years ago. I've been going into prisons ever since. Keynoting conferences, lecturing, and reading my poems at hundreds of universities, prisons, schools, housing projects, ghettos, barrios, reservations, and pueblos—you'll find me there.

It keeps me real, keeps me in touch with those who tell me their stories, and I guess I kind of understand why a friend of mine, Pancho, finds it hard to believe that an immigrant woman would be raped repeatedly by her guards, by ICE, the Homeland Hoodlums.

He reads a lot, is distinguished and respected for his intelligence, he's what you might call a gentrified Chicano. He's well-traveled, well-educated, married to a beautiful white woman, and he's an oratory genius, was the captain of his Yale debate team, and he's so endearing and charming you can't help but love him as I do.

He tells me that not everything is the white man's fault and that a lot of the blame belongs to us, to our laziness, to our unwillingness to go along with the program, that many of us Chicanos are still stuck in the past, history is what it is, what happened happened, that's what invading armies do, they kill the inhabitants and take over and that's what happened, so get on with living.

And I tell him that anytime a crisis occurs, anytime some catastrophe happens in the world, if you read long enough down the column you find a white man at the root of the catastrophe. It's always a corrupt judge, a greedy CEO, a billionaire's lust for power, etc.

And he tells me that if you put a Chicano in the same position, the same thing would likely happen, it's not about ethnic origin, it's about what temptation does to a person who is given the opportunity to have it all. Power corrupts, it doesn't matter who the person is, it just happens that they're white. He accuses me of having a myopic perspective, that I'm too in love with my Chicano origins and people.

His wife, Brandy, is generous, overly giving, hospitable and always ready to accommodate. She's compassionate. I've seen her cry at the pictures on TV of immigrant children taken from their parents. She goes out of her way to feed anyone who walks through her door. And she's always smiling, which bugs me, but I enjoy it.

Pancho doesn't live in the barrio but in an upscale all-white neighborhood. He's been the target of white people wanting him out of their neighborhood but he smiles, finds pleasure in the fact that he rises every morning and goes out to his new hybrid Lexus and waves at their scowling and grim faces.

They don't argue with him anymore or yell that he doesn't belong there, he's too good at speaking English and in seconds pins them down like butterflies in his net in an argument that makes them feel stupid. But that doesn't keep them from throwing trash in his driveway, sometimes even used needles, which he has his immigrant yardman clean up.

When gentrification happens in a neighborhood, the standard argument is to say the poor people are running it down, so the city gives these white developers/envelopers and house buyers monies to fix them up and then white trust-funders move in. That's what Pancho does, he works for the mayor, helping developers take over Chicano barrios.

It's the same in literature, I tell him, a writer of color is shamed and doubted and accused of over-the-top writing when he or she states the injustices happening to them. Teachers don't include her books in the lesson plans, the curriculum banishes such writers, the educational system wants its books nice and clean and white.

Even he claims it's not true, it's exaggeration, and yes, he too wants a clean literature, an antiseptic poetry that treats whites with kid gloves and doesn't look under things to find the dirt. After all, his kids are half white.

He wants them to believe that guards do their duty ethically, that prison rehabilitates, that . . . excuses ad nauseam, I tell him in reply. The unspoken sense is that because he's educated and liberal he must know what's best for us, that his truth is truer than ours, that he sees with wiser eyes and more mature heart. And then he goes on to pull my heart strings until every one of them snaps and I'm almost crying in his lap, almost believing him.

If you're well educated and have a great job, like you, I tell him, then you're not submitted to that barbaric violence. I go to prisons all the time, I see the violence with my own eyes, I tell him. I continue my argument by using an example: even in the face of Weinstein, Rose, and dozens of other sexual predators, even our orange-haired ringmaster swinging from the chandeliers in the oval office preying on women, I mean, after all this, you still believe, I say with incredulous effrontery, our law-'n'-order boys are not criminally inclined?

I'm not saying all of them, I know enough about our dysfunctional prison system and rigged social system to tell you without a doubt, given a chance, the law-'n'-order boy will rape a woman of color quicker than a cat can destroy a roll of toilet paper in her playful paws.

I tell him white people are afraid that whites are going extinct. They're spooked by their self-created fears—I mean, to really believe this you have to be mentally deranged and assailed from all sides by imaginary ghosts that have come back to wreak misery in their souls.

And he says, "No one escapes the Reaper's scythe." And I don't know what the hell he's referring to, and I continue pontificating, "But still, white nationalists insist on blinding themselves to this fact, ignoring all evidence, playing as if our judicial officials are law-abiding. I'll tell you what, my advice to them and to you, Pancho, is don't ever get caught up in the system, then you'll find out firsthand."

"I don't wish that on anyone," he says.

"Well," I continue, "if you doubt me, I wish we could turn invisible and I could take you by the hand so you could witness the horrible things committed daily by our law enforcement people. You wouldn't believe it. But I wouldn't do that, it would have such a negative impact on your way of seeing life that it might traumatize you, my friend. So please trust me when I say it happens— the rapes, the sexual forcing of women to do things by their keepers. This used to be the American experience for the few, for the people of color, for the indigenous; now it's become as common as the national anthem at an athletic spectacle. The American experience for the many."

And he says, "There you go again, way over the top—white supremacist this, white nationalist that—especially the middle class and upper classes, we are at a disadvantage because of our iron-willed insistence to make this a better world, in our belief that it's a just world and people are not tortured or treated inhumanely in America and it stems from the fact that the system upholds and maintains itself despite—now pay attention to my word *despite*—despite these barbaric systems."

He's determined to make-believe that no one escapes justice in the end. No one gets a free pass to escape racism and economic bias. We are all in the same boat.

"Equal opportunity for all, right?" I mock him.

But he slogs on: "How can a system that gives them so much be so bad for others? Democracy is a project in process. We must all work on it daily to make it better, but that doesn't mean if you're treated bad you can just relinquish all responsibility for yourself."

"Yes," I say, "but rather than search for the truth and have the courage to accept it and fight for change, the entitled ones like you prefer the luxury class your skin status gives you, not change."

He says, "It's human folly and you'll find no mouth gaping in shock from me. Injustice is very ho-hum, but a ho-hum nonetheless we must change, for these entitlements you speak of originate in slavery and racism and are practiced and nurtured from our worst and most cruel instincts to dominate others, to satiate our greed, to act superior, to get it all. And we will change that.

"Listen," he continues, "read what Cortez and his soldiers, maddened by gold, God, and greed, did to the indigenous cultures of Latin America and compare it to what oil companies are doing down there. It's the same thing. But the people go along with it. There are those who fight it, there are those who support it. You'll thank me that I helped you realize the errors of your ways my friend. Now come on, let's go to the gym, I have yoga in ten minutes."

On the way he tells me he's reading Terry Tempest Williams's book *Refuge*, and that he received a letter from his mother in Mexico, where she moved recently, and that he's taken up martial arts training.

I tell him, "Your life is filled, Pancho, with money and leisure, and you're not worried about survival."

"I worked for it my friend, never forget that, I worked hard for this lifestyle."

On the way out of the locker room and as we step into the yoga room with mats and mostly women waiting around, I tell him, "You look silly in your yoga spandex. You seem like one of those men in the magazines wearing yoga tights and meditating on some boulder beside a sea."

And as we squat and do sunrise and belly-moon, I whisper to him, "You have a wall between you and the real drudgery of life most of us endure daily. You're telling me, come, I invite you to have this great life, look at me, running five miles in the morning, nice house, nice clothes, great food, you can do this too. And all I get out of it is a pulled hamstring."

30.
—

Chicano Refuge

I AM WRITING THIS FROM MY CABIN IN NORTHERN NEW MEXICO. Behind my place, to the east are cliffs O'Keeffe painted and sold for millions to the Kemper Museum in Kansas. To the west, La Princesa, to the north the Red Valley, a wide-open scorched basin where thousands of wild horses used to roam, to the south the Santa Fe National Forest with hundreds of springs lashing the leafy ground with winding streams.

I make buttered toast for my dog, and when I let her out to eat I catch sight of a big white-tailed buck standing before me—a second later it's gone, flashing off behind sage and dogwood, and in another blink my dog darts after it between trees, both dashing in the bramble up the hill and vanishing into the forest.

Standing on the porch (*el portal*), I wave to my neighbor, a friend I have hardly spoken a few words to in twenty years. I like it that way. We nod. We wave. We pass each other at a distance wordlessly, treasure the silence of the canyon. The silence here is the underlying foundation of all that exists. Here even the rocks and boulders breathe. They're like old men and women making themselves forever available to the stories of rain, wind, sunlight, flowers breaking through in the field. I've been told by several healers that this canyon, shaped like a V, is a sacred vagina where Mother Earth works her charms on all that lives. It awakened in me over the years a love for myself, for the way my legs move down a trail in the forest. When I drink the water pulsing from a spring, I can taste Mother's juices renewing my muscles and heart. I can sense the air course through my lungs and veins, lifting a sadness in me. I can see all manner of flowers and trees and believe in the magic and power of this place to heal me.

There are certain white men who know this power, who are part of the human family, who have done their work, and their hearts are as mine, filled with reverence for the land. They hear it too in their bones, sense the slight crunch of footsteps of spirit ancestors who centuries before walked the path they now tread with love for all living things.

It was this place that convinced me to go back into prisons and teach inmates how to read and write, this place that taught me to serve those in prison, to carry books in and hand them out, to arouse in the convict a sense of worth, to repair the tattered soul, to believe in the heart again. This place, where one waits on things to appear, waits to hear the voice of trees, listens intently to the murmuring in the brush, the bird echoes orchestrating in canyons, here one waits with the alertness of eyes that roam the land as a child's eyes might imagine a magical land in a cluster of boulders where the water pours over ivy and towering pines look down like ancient gods guffawing with laughter. All of it, even the stars at night that emerge brilliant and solitary and diamond-bright, close to the face, almost ready to give birth in my soul to some distinct presence that harbors itself therein, waiting, waiting until I am ready to receive and understand it.

Because I deal with white supremacy and may impress the reader with a distasteful attitude, lest you think me a cynical ogre hemorrhaging bitterness, nay, far from it—I simply experience this and then go out into the world and suffer the unimaginable hatred of white supremacists for the essence of life, and so I speak; but let me hasten to add not all people who work in the prison system or youth authority confinement areas are bad. I've met amazing people, and they are special, I don't mean to flatter them. Anthony the warden was one of them. One of the best, willing to go out of his way to seek and develop programs for inmates under his care.

In the beginning when I started visiting prisons again, I was conflicted from the moment I stepped into the facility, and I could hear the voices of fellow writers and poets at literary conferences where we sat around tables drinking whiskey and they told me, "You can't keep going back to prison to work with them. Your time is too valuable. Write your poems. Forget the cons. Your work with them lessens the literary merit of your work, lessens your stature and esteem as a poet. People will start to think your writing is only as good as your activism in prison. In other words, you won't be a pure writer. Did Paz go into prisons? Did Faulkner? Hemingway? No."

They meant for me and my work to be considered truly literary, and not fall into the category of social worker or political hack, these two latter strains in their eyes deflating the worth of my work as somehow not real poetry or not real literature. They meant well, meaning they thought I was wasting my time with prisoners and teaching them to read and write, that I should stay home and focus on the work, send it to my agent, publish it and stay out of the business of helping others. They thought my activism belittled my work. Their hearts, as I said, were in the right place, they wanted me to be considered a poet apart from my work with prisoners, a writer separate from my concerns on injustice.

(Tell me why Sister Helen Prejean and Father Greg from Homeboy Industries are never told their work with illiterates and street addicts detracts from their status as writers—no indeed, they're good writers *because* of their work in prisons. Again, only people of color have to endure the double standard.)

And though that may be the history of writers and poets in this country, in almost every other country in the world, poets go to prison, poets work with prisoners. Only in America is it considered beneath a poet.

It's a way of whitewashing literature, of making it so we don't blemish the ice-cream-and-cupcake smeared lips of readers who don't want to be bothered with what's on the other side of the fence. The establishment wants to encourage a kind of poetry that only speaks of sweet things.

But I couldn't. Because part of the America I know and millions of others know is not kind, is not a just and tempered America. It's vicious and savage and devours the innocent. It was part of my life. I had learned to write in prison, serving a six-to-fifty-year sentence for drug possession with the intent to distribute. I saw America undressed in its scabrous and leprous ugly flesh. I saw it condemn the young, execute the innocent, banish to dark realms kids who had only made bad choices.

I wondered about compassion the day I first went in, seeing the cons in their pods in their boxer shorts, their tattoos, their distrustful looks, their brazen effrontery to all that was decent. The place smelled rancid. The sounds grated against my nerves. The guards with keys and walkie-talkies and the inhuman glaze of the concrete corridors bothered me, and fear swept through me, forgotten memories flared and sizzled up my spine with hatred for them and the filthy place, and I regretted my ridiculous empathy.

What a fool I was to think I could change anything! What a proud and egotistical clown to believe I could do good here. Nonetheless, I kept going in until this beautiful place I write from this morning, March 24, 2019, clashed with the prison conditions, and from the contrast arose an understanding of myself, deeper and on many levels, that I needed to do this for me.

At times, after leaving a prison, I have an urge to do drugs, and I regret coming in—a remorseful voice in my head keeps repeating, I should have listened to my writer and poet friends. I need to forget the prison system, the prisoners, this whole, ugly mess and become a tourist poet, writing only about pretty brochure things, someone who writes about the sweet life, China visits, abstract responses to Pollock's paintings, family matters, identity issues, man/woman relationship issues, don my blue hat and vest and suit coat and parade on stage combing my fingers through the fur of an expensive poodle on my lap.

But the question always nags at me: why be a fraud now? Why affect a foreign accent and limp wrist and curtsey before the poetry reader, the booksellers, setting them at ease that I will not rock the boat, that I am a "nice" Spaniard, that I love Taco Bell and refuse to speak Mexican or Chicano slang, that I am a "Spanish" man, that you can be assured I have turned my back on my experience as an oppressed man of color, an indigenous warrior and poet, that I am as white as a clean sheet of typing paper, that my cultural ties to my Indo-Chicano heritage are as extinct as the ten-winged blue butterfly or African white rhino. I have been thoroughly cleaned of my Chicanismo, of any trace of defiance and challenge, that I am one of those poets who marry a girl with money and I speak in whispers and move elegantly and charm my listeners as a literary enigma, processed and acceptable procedurally as string cheese and wine on a balcony table overlooking the River Seine in Paris.

I tried. Got the suit, bought a nice pad, got on all the right philanthropy boards, wrote sweet poems, never turned back to look at the homeless or at the prison a half hour's drive from the plaza; I forgot about Los Alamos, where scientists devise killing weapons, never talk about the racism, never allude to the injustice of rich kids' parents paying their children's way into elite colleges by bribing admissions administrators or paying someone to take the test for their kids or paying for the answer sheet.

I tried. But I couldn't keep my charm up, couldn't keep aloof from the distasteful, got tired of merrily raising my wine glass with old women and men toasting how great life was in the upper crust.

Eventually I returned to tortillas, to manual labor, to driving to prisons, to visiting schools lacking teachers, to collecting and handing out books. I couldn't continue the other life, couldn't keep the sitcom going, couldn't hum in ashrams anymore with trust-funders, couldn't do yoga anymore or write quaint articles on travel, couldn't read Buddhist books, practicing tai chi every morning and martial arts every evening, camera slung around my neck, dashing off for my Thai massage, quoting Rumi.

I went back to being a literary outlaw.

And I don't disrespect those who pursue a crystalline literary life, nay, all power to them. Why? Because there is absolutely nothing wrong with this. And I wish all who want to venture in this direction do so with as many blessings showering their sweet heads as blossoms from Japanese cherry trees in the spring.

But I was never good at doing things the easy way. And to be honest, I wasn't sure what I was more afraid of—wearing a suit and standing next to a whole bunch of rich old white men in suits on stage, part of a distinguished literary board, or later, after the toothy grins and money awards, finding that the same white men are proven false, frauds, predators feeding off women of color. So I returned to the fetid halls of youth authority, to find myself yet again standing front and center with a bunch of juvies charged and found guilty of committing robberies and murder and burglaries, each facing the camera holding a book of mine, smiling, recognizing this opportunity, this moment, as one that can change their lives forever.

31.

—

Algo paso

So what happened between the years I wrote the essays in *Working in the Dark* and this journal entry? Well, perhaps I must admit that I'm caught between the two. Rather than expatriate myself to a nice Mexican resort as a Diego Rivera impostor with Frida Kahlo on my arm, I built a cabin in the forest and retreat here whenever I have the opportunity. Bears, lions, eagles, rattlers, turkey, fish, trees, vultures. They are much better at teaching me mindfulness than all the oracles clutching their iPhones and listening to Siri's advice.

When I look back over *Working in the Dark*, I almost want to reach out and hug that man I was. The world has changed so much since *Working in the Dark* and *Blood In/Blood Out* came out. At the time I thought I knew myself, knew the world a little, but looking behind me I see a man driven by the madness of wanting to do right in the world and failing at every turn. I see a man who listened more to the ocean's waves than Hollywood producers. I stayed in bed reading Richard Wright or Seamus Heaney, listening to gypsy music, ignoring every social networking event to isolate myself among words and sea waves. I find it odd now that I report on my own life in *Working in the Dark* as if my life is alien to me, as if another man is living it and I'm reporting from the sidelines, as if we are two men, one who lives this crazy, sometimes death-risking outlaw life and the other a sedentary meditative life.

Working in prisons teaching men and women to read and write is a case in point. In a couple of hours I will hike a trail into the forest and pause awestruck by a mushroom, a lichen on a log, the way streams sparkle and cross the trail.

The essence of being a prisoner and a poet is when the image catches you and sets fire to every blade of dry grass in your heart. You're caught blindly moving through invisible flames. You're in the greatest adventure of your life, each line is a death-defying cliff leap, each word arranged against another word is nourishment to a starving man, each paragraph is a glistening cup of cold water to a man coming in from a week under the blazing sun in a desert.

I mean that being in an environment of life and death, where other cons can take you out, where guards can do whatever they want, where your writing is a sailboat caught in a storm and you're supposed to cross this raging sea of time with no compass or map—this environment offers one of the greatest adventures you will ever have. So to expect anyone living in such an intense atmosphere to be content with going back to a bill-paying life, getting up and going to work, stepping into a social limbo of sorts, where life is faint and the glimmer of high adventure nonexistent, is absurd.

At least for me it was. I could adjust. I could cope with the slow motion of life. To planning, to waiting for my Friday check—it meant nothing to me, I wanted the poem back, I wanted to feel the burn again, to run my thumb along the sharp blade of a verb, to find myself in momentary ecstasy over an image that grew from a spontaneous combustion of an arrangement of words.

It's like asking a concert violinist to play Mozart on a yo-yo string. And I had trouble doing that. So when I walked into the facility, I again heard the violin, stirring in my heart, again the five hundred musicians tuning their instruments of life and death, and ahh—I found myself remembering the grand concert halls and the standing applause of thousands of words after a day of writing.

Writing poetry and reading novels and poetry was where the real action was. It was the toughest routine I ever submitted myself to, the excruciating moment when a word or sentence or image grabbed something inside me, a memory that was dormant and hiding beneath the plow's blades, and it raked it up, and I cried, my tears dripping onto the page, feeling no longer, for a moment, like a stranger to myself, feeling I had come, if only in an effervescent moment in time—to myself again. And it's strange to say, but for a man who rarely weeps, I've learned over time that only in tears do I catch a glimpse of who I really am, do I get really close to what I'm feeling about my life.

On the page, shaking like dice the magical cluster of god bones and angel gristle we call words, I let them fly out. As parts of me dueled between death and life like bloody gladiators, this page was where my heart entered naked and vulnerable and on this page as sure and certain as any street or glimmering swimming pool, the lover in me was run down by some tweaked-out meth head and died and was drowned by what glimmered like inviting wealth, as I realized how mean and selfish people were; and here, the thief I was and the arrogant man I was were conquered by a single word, some blue-finned swordfish that paused midair in my breath, wildly flailing my beauty and sound of my voice and the gods got angry that I had defied them and taken a bite of the forbidden fruit—yes, the Roman Coliseum was nothing compared to a stanza of poetry!

And I grew addicted to such drama, so when I stopped writing, which I did on my release, I was looking for something with that much adrenaline and so drifted gradually into drugs and outlaws' company hoping it might cure my fever a bit, but it never did.

And as the months progressed into years, the winters into springs and summers and autumns, I withdrew into ever-darkening circles of hell, waiting, waiting for something to spark me alive again, leaving behind my writing, my books, mindlessly I went on, refusing to call anyone for help.

Perhaps what the *Working in the Dark* essays never dealt with sufficiently is my mother being murdered, shot five times in the face with a .45 by her husband, or maybe my father dying in a gutter in San Francisco. I had never grieved them, never even wept at their funerals, because I never attended their funerals. And even when someone tried to talk sense to me, to stop me from my descent into the oblivion of drugs and whiskey and outlaw life, I ignored them—in fact, I stayed as far away from people who were trying to help as I could. I needed destruction, I needed to burn myself on the pyre of not caring, I needed to kill the gift in me because it demanded too much. And I couldn't tame it, moderate it, feed it in measured cups to the world, it was consuming me—"kill the gift, motherfucker, kill the gift" was my mantra, do it by fucking strange women all night, by doing drugs every day, kill it by riding my Harley over a hundred miles an hour knowing at any moment I would lose control. Kill the gift. I wanted to kill it and assume a different identity, cannon into another world, into another universe, and observe life from the place where fleshless spirits live. Go back, back, back, into mother's womb, back to sperm and mother's egg, back to being a nothingness particle in the universe, so I could see myself emanating as sunlight, so I was empty of disturbing memories from the orphanage that haunted me, so the cruelty of remembering would be gone, and just be energy, only energy, part of every living atom everything was composed of.